DARK HORSES
ANNUAL 2017

DARK
HORSES
ANNUAL 2017

MARTEN JULIAN

Raceform

Published in 2017 by Raceform

27 Kingfisher Court, Hambridge Road, Newbury RG14 5SJ

Copyright © Marten Julian 2017

The right of Marten Julian to be identified as the author of this work has been asserted by him in accordance with the Copyright, Designs and Patents Act 1988.

A catalogue record for this book is available from the British Library.

ISBN 978-1-910497-27-2

Designed by Fiona Pike

Printed and bound in the UK by CPI Group (UK) Ltd, Croydon, CR0 4YY

CONTENTS

Keep in touch

If you want to keep in touch with Marten's thoughts on a regular basis then read his free-to-view journal at:

www.martenjulian.com

or ring him on:

0906 150 1555

Selections given in the first minute

(calls charged at £1.50 a minute at all times)

Follow Marten

 @martenjulian

INTRODUCTION

Hi there!

Thank you for buying the 2017 edition of the *Dark Horses Annual*.

I hope that you find this book a useful source of reference and enjoyment through the course of the season. If you are buying the book for the first time here is a brief guide as to how the horses have been selected.

My qualifiers for the Premier List are chosen in the hope and expectation that they will have rewarded support to level stakes by the end of the season. It is my belief that they possess the specific attributes that merit our special interest.

The selections in the Dark Horses feature are generally lightly raced, unexposed or unraced types with more of a long-term future.

This season I have also included a section devoted to a handful of lightly-raced horses that I believe were campaigned last season with handicaps uppermost in mind. I have also devoted a section, for the first time this year, to well-regarded, unraced and lightly-raced Irish horses.

Please note that as the deadline for the book is late March, any news since then will be unaccounted for. Unfortunately, entries for the Oaks were not available at the time of writing.

You can keep in touch with my latest thoughts about the horses featured in this book either through my *Weekend Card*, which updates the progress of the Premier List horses every week, or by ringing my line, which is updated every day (0906 150 1555). For further details of a subscription or text-based service please ring Rebecca (01539 741007) or contact her by email (rebecca@ martenjulian.com).

I am, as always, indebted to Rebecca, Julian Brown, James Norris, Jodie Standing, Ian Greensill and Paul Day for their help at various stages of this production.

Finally, I would like to wish you the very best of good fortune for the season.

Bye for now.

Marten Julian

the Weekend card

For as little as £5 a week!

What's it all about...

After over 40 years in the business Marten and his team get to hear a lot from clients about what they're after from a service, which is why we see it as a priority to cater for as many of their needs as possible. That is the reason why last July we brought back *the Weekend Card,* which was our best-selling service many years ago, and as you can see from the published results it has proved a huge success since its return.

Continuity...

One thing that has become clear is the importance of *continuity* in a service. For example, when we select a horse we know that our clients would appreciate some feedback — whether it wins or loses. *The Weekend Card* prioritises this by providing weekly updates on key horses from Marten's ***Dark Horses Annuals*** (both Flat and Jumps), selected horses from earlier editions and features of the Weekend Card and horses that received special mention in the Postscript Service.

The Contents...

The Weekend Card includes the following features:

- **The Sleeper Section** — one of the most popular features of *the Weekend Card,* with Marten's specially noted horses — a few dark ones, a few unexposed ones and a few unraced ones.
- **The Clock Watcher** — Marten has devised a system to identify horses that have put up exceptional performances on the clock.

- **The Ante-Post Agenda** — a brief weekly update on horses that Marten believes warrant ante-post interest. Again, there will be continuity of mention.
- **Under The Radar** — observations, sometimes controversial, from Marten on subjects that the pundits miss — or choose to avoid! Strange rides, stable news and other intriguing issues!
- **The Weekend Action** — the Weekend Card covers Marten's thoughts on the big-race action at the weekend, together with horses that have caught his eye elsewhere.
- **The Update** — latest news and entries for horses that have featured in past *Weekend Cards*, the *Dark Horses Annuals* and the *Postscript Service*.
- **Ian Carnaby** — a great favourite of our clients and a big part of our team for many years.
- **Jodie's Jottings** — Marten's assistant Jodie Standing specialises in Irish point-to-pointers but she will also be sharing her occasional insights from the Flat.
- **The Irish Angle** — observations and informed comment from over the water!
- **The Results...**

We believe that the only fair way to assess any service is by recording and updating the returns to a one point level stake and also as a percentage return on investment.

If you would like a full explanation of how these returns are calculated, or a complete list of results, then please contact Rebecca (rebecca@martenjulian.com).

Here are the returns for the period from July 2016 to the end of February 2017

Marten's Weekend Action 58% profit on investment (43pts LSP) including winners at 22/1, 14/1, 11/1, 8/1 (twice), 7/1, 6/1 (three times) etc

The Sleeper Section 120% profit on investment (31pts LSP) including winners at 33/1, 7/1, 7/2 etc

Under The Radar 18% profit on investment (3pts LSP) including winners at 7/1, 11/2 etc

Jodie's Jottings 56% profit on investment (32pts LSP) including winners at 14/1 (twice), 8/1, 6/1, 5/1 etc

Ian Carnaby 4% profit on investment (3pts LSP) including winners at 16/1, 6/1, 11/2, 5/1 etc

THE PREMIER HORSES

The following dozen horses have been selected in the expectation that they will reward support through the course of the season.

CHESSMAN (3YR BAY COLT)

TRAINER:	**John Gosden**
FORM:	**1 -**
PEDIGREE:	**Acclamation – Dulcian (Shamardal)**
BHA RATING:	—
OPTIMUM TRIP:	**1m**

Set the pulse racing by the manner of his success on his debut in a 7f maiden at Kempton in November.

Last of the 13 runners on the turn for home, having missed the break, he weaved his way through the field on the bridle to quicken and win very easily by two and a quarter lengths. The form of the race has not held up – the third was beaten twice subsequently and is rated on 69 – but the winner could not have been more impressive.

This colt has plenty of speed in his pedigree, by the sprinter Acclamation out of an unraced half-sister to Cheveley Park winner Serious Attitude from the family of top-class two-year-old Mount Abu.

He stayed the seven furlongs well at Kempton but is not certain to appreciate much further.

Likely to be placed in a handicap initially but expected to progress to better things. Has a fast-ground bias to his pedigree.

CORONET (3YR GREY FILLY)

TRAINER:	John Gosden
FORM:	11 -
PEDIGREE:	Dubawi – Approach (Darshaan)
BHA RATING:	99
OPTIMUM TRIP:	1m 4f

It is all about stamina with this daughter of Dubawi, who is crying out for a mile and a half.

She overcame clear signs of inexperience to beat Alwaysandforever on her racecourse debut in an extended 1m maiden fillies' stakes at Leicester in September, the slow pace against her but displaying an emphatic turn of foot two furlongs from home to sweep clear of her rivals and win eased down by half a length.

She was stepped up to a mile and a quarter just over a month later against the colts in the Listed Zetland Stakes at

Coronet – very tough and looks sure to stay the Oaks trip

Newmarket. Once again green in the early stages, but she took closer order two furlongs from home and squeezed through to take up the running inside the final furlong, needing firm driving to hold the late challenge of her 97-rated stable-companion Cunco by a neck, with the 91-rated Permian a further half-length away in third.

Coronet is the eighth foal of her dam, a Listed winner for Sir Mark Prescott over 1m 2f and a half-sister to French Guineas winner Aussie Rules. She is a half-sister to four winners including 1m 2f Group 2 winner and St Leger runner-up Midas Touch and 1m 2f winner Streetcar To Stars.

Coronet has the ideal profile for the Oaks. She is sure to stay the trip and has already established a reasonable level of form. The trainer says the plan is to start her at York in the Musidora Stakes in the hope that she acquits herself well enough to go to Epsom.

CRYSTAL OCEAN (3YR BAY COLT)

TRAINER:	**Sir Michael Stoute**
FORM:	**2 -**
PEDIGREE:	**Sea The Stars – Crystal Star (Mark Of Esteem)**
BHA RATING:	**—**
OPTIMUM TRIP:	**1m 2f +**

It is now accepted that Sir Michael Stoute does not expect his two-year-old debutants to receive a hard race on their debuts.

Generally the more talented ones show up well for much of the race before tiring close home, while those that are less able do just enough to learn something about racing. The key, though, is that they all have an enjoyable experience.

This was evident in the case of Crystal Ocean, who made his debut in a 7f maiden at Newbury in September. The son of Sea The Stars was the subject of upbeat reports beforehand, a view reflected in his starting 7/4 favourite. Steadily away, he progressed from halfway and may have taken the lead for a few strides before getting caught close home and beaten a neck by the once-raced Warrior's Spirit.

On paper the form is nothing special, with the winner subsequently rated on 81 and On To Victory, a head away in third, rated on 75. That would put Crystal Ocean on a mark in the high 70s – a long way below Pattern-class standard.

Crystal Ocean, the seventh foal of her dam, comes from one of her owner's most successful lines. He is a three-parts brother to 1m 4f Group 2 winner Crystal Capella, a winner of eight races, and half-brother to the tough Hillstar, winner of the Grade 1 Canadian International Stakes, last season's talented but eventually disappointing Crystal Zvezda and Sandor, a winner up to 1m 2f.

Crystal Ocean should win his maiden, probably over a mile or more, but the hope is that he can work his way up to better things through the handicap route.

DAL HARRAILD (4YR CHESTNUT GELDING)

TRAINER:	**William Haggas**
FORM:	**4212/013131 -**
PEDIGREE:	**Champs Elysees – Dalvina (Grand Lodge)**
BHA RATING:	**109**
OPTIMUM TRIP:	**1m 4f +**

This strong son of Champs Elysees displayed steady improvement as a two and three-year-old and was still

Dal Harraild – a prospective Group-class performer

progressing towards the end of last season, rising from a mark of 87 in April to 109 by the autumn.

He shaped well at two, finishing fourth and second before responding well to firm driving to beat Replenish by a length at Haydock in September. He ran second beaten a neck just over a month later from a mark of 83 in a 1m 1f nursery at Nottingham.

He ran the one poor race of his career when tailed off on his return at Sandown last April, but returned to form next time out in June, landing a valuable extended 1m 4f 0-90 handicap at Musselburgh by two and a quarter lengths from a mark of 87.

Dal Harraild did very well to run a close third off 95 in a 0-105 1m 4f handicap at Ascot in July after being held up in last and then blocked when trying to get a run two furlongs out. He gained compensation for that misfortune when staying on well to beat Shraaoh by a short-head off 98 in a valuable 1m 4f handicap at Goodwood.

He looked sure to win next time at Ascot, travelling very

easily two furlongs out, but was then unable to respond when challenged by New Caledonia, going down by two and a quarter lengths in third off 102. Raised in class next time for a Listed race at Newmarket, he made all to beat the useful 110-rated Barsanti by two and a quarter lengths, staying on powerfully to the line.

He is very well suited to fast ground and seemed to enjoy making the running at Newmarket. Now proven at Listed level and he looks more than capable of taking a Group race.

Most progressive and has not stopped improving yet and one to keep in mind for a midsummer Group contest on fast ground. Stays a mile and a half very well and may get further.

MAKE TIME (3YR CHESTNUT COLT)

TRAINER:	**David Menuisier**
FORM:	**21 -**
PEDIGREE:	**Makfi – Poppet's Lovein (Lomitas)**
BHA RATING:	**91**
OPTIMUM TRIP:	**1m 2f +**

Make Time is one of the most interesting horses in this section.

He ran a blinder on his debut in a 7f maiden at Ascot in September, in arrears after a slow start before making steady headway to take the lead entering the final furlong under hands and heels riding only to be pipped on the line by Frontispiece.

The son of Makfi impressed greatly later in the month in a 7f maiden run in soft ground at Salisbury, up there from the outset before leading two furlongs out and quickening discernibly to pull five lengths clear of Swiftsure and win with plenty in hand in a good time. The subsequent form of the race worked out quite well.

He is the second foal of a winning half-sister to 6f Group 2

winner Overdose from the family of 1m 4f Group 3 winner
Upend.

Make Time showed both good pace and an ability to change
gear last season, handling the soft ground well at Salisbury
having coped with quicker conditions on his debut.

He is already useful, with the potential to become a Pattern-
class performer. Very exciting.

MIRAGE DANCER (3YR BAY COLT)

TRAINER:	**Sir Michael Stoute**
FORM:	**1 -**
PEDIGREE:	**Frankel – Heat Haze (Green Desert)**
BHA RATING:	**87**
OPTIMUM TRIP:	**1m**

This colt took an eternity to find his stride when winning a 7f
maiden at Doncaster in October but his reputation is such that
he merits inclusion in this feature.

Steadily away from the stalls and already being shuffled along
at halfway, he required serious urgings from the saddle to make
up ground on the leaders. Still only third and looking one-paced
a furlong out, he then found his stride to get up close home and
win by half-a-length from Tafaakhor.

The form is mixed, with the runner-up a nine-race maiden
currently rated on 85 in late March, but the third a winner next
time and the fourth useful.

Mirage Dancer is by Frankel and a half-brother to useful
performers Forge and Radiator. His dam was a Grade 1 winner
up to an extended 9f and a half-sister to Dansili, Banks Hill and
other high-class performers.

Mirage Dancer – rated highly by his trainer

This colt comes from a very talented family but both his half-brother and half-sister slightly underachieved, so a note of caution is advised. He does, though, enjoy a tall reputation in the yard and there was much to like about his willing attitude at Doncaster once the penny dropped.

He may struggle to stay much beyond a mile.

PIVOINE (3YR BAY COLT)

TRAINER:	Sir Michael Stoute
FORM:	31 -
PEDIGREE:	Redoute's Choice – Fleur De Cactus (Montjeu)
BHA RATING:	82
OPTIMUM TRIP:	1m 2f +

Pivoine was beaten a long way when third of eight behind Via Egnatia on his debut at Newmarket in October, staying on steadily at one pace to the line.

He was much improved later in the month, winning a 1m maiden at Kempton pulling clear by two and a half lengths. Well away from the stalls, he raced handily in second until the straight, but looked outpaced for a few strides two furlongs from home. He then found his stride and showed a hint of a turn of foot to pass his rivals and pull clear once his stamina kicked in.

Pivoine is the first foal of a 1m 5f winning half-sister to Listed placed Red Dune from the family of Fiorente, formerly trained in this yard before winning the Melbourne Cup, and related to top-class Group 1 winners Islington and Hellenic.

The Kempton form looks only ordinary – the runner-up, third and fourth were all beaten next time – but he comes from a slow-maturing family that the trainer knows very well.

He is likely to work his way up through handicaps before progressing to better grade races in the autumn. He is bred to be particularly effective at a mile and a half or more.

POET'S WORD (4YR BAY COLT)

TRAINER:	**Sir Michael Stoute**
FORM:	**4/31412 -**
PEDIGREE:	**Poet's Voice – Whirly Bird (Nashwan)**
BHA RATING:	**104**
OPTIMUM TRIP:	**1m 2f +**

Poet's Word has the perfect profile for a horse trained in this yard.

A promising fourth in a 7f maiden on his sole start at two, he returned last season with a third in a 1m maiden at Chelmsford followed by a victory in a 1m 2f maiden on good to firm ground at Nottingham. There was much to like about the way he won there, travelling comfortably just behind the leaders before staying on strongly to hold Muntahaa – rated 113 at the end of the season – by two and a quarter lengths at the line.

That form worked out well, with the runner-up winning twice subsequently and finishing fourth in the St Leger, the third Shraaoh winning next time out and the fourth, fifth and seventh also subsequently successful.

Poet's Word was then beaten from a mark of 87 on good to soft ground at Epsom before returning to form in good style in a 1m 3f 0-90 handicap at Goodwood back on good to firm ground from a mark of 88. Well placed in fifth turning for home, he was caught flat-footed as the pace quickened two furlongs from home before finding his stride and going clear to win by a length and a quarter from Sixties Groove.

Poet's Word ran well on his final start of the season from a 10lb higher mark at Doncaster, finishing second to Central Square after being squeezed for room in the final furlong.

This immensely likeable colt is the sixth foal of Whirly Bird, a very progressive and tough daughter of Nashwan and a half-

Poet's Word – destined for Group-class company

sister to 1m 6f Group 3 winner Ursa Major. At stud she has produced Group 3 winner Malabar, 7f winner Whirly Dancer, staying winner Royal Signaller and Clowance Estate, a winner up to 1m 3f.

Everything about Poet's Word suggests he is crying out for a step up to a mile and a half. It was only inside the final furlong that he got going at Goodwood while his other requirement is quick ground.

Currently rated on 104, he is perfectly poised to win another top handicap before progressing to Pattern-class level. I urge you to keep on the right side of this progressive colt especially when he is asked to tackle middle distances on the fast summer ground. Black type awaits him.

RED LABEL (3YR BAY COLT)

TRAINER:	**Luca Cumani**
FORM:	**31 -**
PEDIGREE:	**Dubawi – Born Something (Caerleon)**
BHA RATING:	**81**
OPTIMUM TRIP:	**1m 2f +**

This son of Dubawi shaped well when third of ten to Time Zone in a 7f maiden on his debut at Newmarket in September.

He appeared the following month in an extended 1m maiden at Leicester, well away racing in fourth and looking outpaced two furlongs from home. Bustled along, he responded well to draw alongside X Rated before pulling clear to win cosily by one and a quarter lengths.

Not cheap at 375,000gns as a yearling, he is a half-brother to 1m 2f winner Tarbawi and 1m winner Best Example. His dam, who was Group-placed around a mile, is from the family of the world-class miler Goldikova.

Red Label is bred to stay at least a mile and a quarter and certainly looked to need a trip last season. He is likely to be brought along steadily by his astute handler, probably working his way through the handicap route.

RICHIE McCAW (4YR BAY GELDING)

TRAINER:	**Ian Williams**
FORM:	**51/344 -**
PEDIGREE:	**Zamindar – Cochin (Swain)**
BHA RATING:	**77**
OPTIMUM TRIP:	**1m 2f +**

This lightly-raced gelding shaped last season as if he had more to offer, notably when fourth of eight beaten a length in a 1m

Ian Williams – a talented dual-purpose handler

2f 0-85 handicap at Sandown in September. Held up behind, he looked one-paced two furlongs out until staying on up the rising ground inside the final furlong.

He then reappeared the following month in an extended 1m 2f 0-85 at York but failed to respond in the closing stages, finishing fourth.

Formerly trained by Mark Johnston, he won the second of his two starts at two when making all to land a 1m maiden at Chelmsford by two lengths from Gold Trade.

He is the eighth foal of his dam and a half-brother to winners over a mile and a half and a mile and three-quarters. His dam is related to a Grade 1 winner over 1m 3f from the family of Xaar.

There may be risks attached but Richie McCaw is included here in the belief that he will improve when stepped up to a mile and a half, a trip he is bred to relish.

TEMPLE CHURCH (3YR BAY COLT)

TRAINER:	**Hughie Morrison**
FORM:	**31 -**
PEDIGREE:	**Lawman – All Hallows (Dalakhani)**
BHA RATING:	**96**
OPTIMUM TRIP:	**1m 2f +**

Temple Church overcame clear signs of greenness when holding on bravely to beat Raheen House by a neck in the prestigious Haynes, Hanson & Clark Conditions Race at Newbury in September, chasing the leader for much of the race until taking up the running approaching the final furlong. He then maintained the gallop despite wandering, both left and right, and held on well to win all out.

Temple Church had run third of 11 on his debut at the same

Temple Church – a high-class stayer in the making

track in August, looking one-paced in the closing stages.

The form of the Newbury race worked out well, with the runner-up next time finishing a very creditable fourth to Rivet in the Group 1 Racing Post Trophy.

Temple Church did extremely well to show such ability at two given the stoutness of his pedigree. He is the second foal of his dam and a full brother to the fair stayer Argyle, out of an unraced half-sister to French Leger winner Allegretto, out of 2m 2f Doncaster Cup winner Alleluia.

This promising colt, who is bred to stay at least a mile and a half, now looks exceptionally well bought at 27,000gns as a yearling, and may be one to keep in mind for top-class back-end staying races, perhaps warranting a crack at the St Leger.

Sir Michael Stoute – the master

ZAINHOM (3YR CHESTNUT COLT)

TRAINER:	**Sir Michael Stoute**
FORM:	**312 -**
PEDIGREE:	**Street Cry – Kaseema (Storm Cat)**
BHA RATING:	**109**
OPTIMUM TRIP:	**1m +**

This intriguing colt did extremely well to show such useful form at two given his obvious signs of immaturity.

Having run a fair third on his debut at Leicester in August, he then improved markedly to win a 7f maiden a month later at York despite running very green throughout and taking a while to pick up. Well on top at the finish, the form was upheld by the second and third, both subsequent winners.

He was stepped up in grade just over a month later for the Group 3 Autumn Stakes at Newmarket. Again, looking very inexperienced throughout the race, he was behind early on and then short of room when trying to come with a challenge on the rising ground, staying on very well once clear despite holding his head at quite a high angle.

Zainhom is the fifth foal of a mare that won over six furlongs at two, from the family of US Grade 1 miling winner Aragorn and One Cool Cat.

This is the sort of colt who could go either way, but he could not be in better hands to realise his true potential and he probably has the ability to win at Group level.

If you want to keep in touch with Marten's thoughts on a regular basis then read his free-to-view journal at:

www.martenjulian.com

or ring him on:

0906 150 1555

Selections given in the first minute

 @martenjulian

THE DARK HANDICAPPERS

The following horses have left the impression that they were trained last season with handicaps uppermost in mind.

AELIUS (3YR CHESTNUT GELDING)

TRAINER:	Michael Easterby
FORM:	00 -
PEDIGREE:	Sepoy – Syvilla (Nayef)
BHA RATING:	—
OPTIMUM TRIP:	1m

Leaves the impression that he has a whole heap of latent ability, revealed notably when he made strong late headway to finish fifth of 12 to Kruger Park on his debut in a decent maiden at York over an extended five furlongs in September.

Less eye-catching back there just over a month later, finishing ninth of 13 to Gulliver keeping on at one pace.

Third foal and a half-brother to Ruler Of France, a winner around a mile, and French 1m 4f and 2m 1f hurdle winner Mavilla. Dam Listed placed over middle distances.

Probably the best three-year-old in the yard and has sufficient ability to win a maiden if wanted, but more likely to have a third run for a handicap mark. Optimum trip uncertain, but may stay a mile.

Probably useful.

BEARAG (3YR BAY FILLY)

TRAINER:	**David O'Meara**
FORM:	**043 -**
PEDIGREE:	**Dutch Art – Cats Eyes (Echo Of Light)**
BHA RATING:	**64**
OPTIMUM TRIP:	**1m +**

May not be anything too special, but shaped quite well on her last two starts over six furlongs given that she is bred to stay further.

Not disgraced when beaten four lengths on her debut in a 5f maiden at Beverley in September. Kept on well next time after coming under pressure at halfway when fourth of 14 in a 6f maiden at Newcastle. Returned to the course and distance in October, staying on steadily to finish third of 11.

Not cheap at 110,000gns as a yearling, she is the first foal of a 5f winning half-sister to 7f Listed winner Nufoos by Echo Of Light.

In the right hands to exploit what could be a reasonable mark for handicaps.

BENJAMIN THOMAS (3YR BAY GELDING)

TRAINER:	**John Quinn**
FORM:	**22 -**
PEDIGREE:	**Mayson – Strudel (Spectrum)**
BHA RATING:	—
OPTIMUM TRIP:	**1m +**

Displayed a plucky attitude in his two runs, staying on after showing bright early speed in a 6f maiden at Pontefract on his debut in September and then just failing to catch Lucky Mistake over the same course and distance the following month.

Fifth foal of a 1m 2f winning daughter of Spectrum from the family of 1m 4f Group 2 winner and St Leger third Bonny Scot.

Comes from a stout and late-developing family on his dam's side so did well to show such pace over six furlongs.

Bred to thrive over a mile or more and heading for a mark in the low 70s on lines taken through his second race.

One to note for a decent midseason handicap over a mile or thereabouts.

BOLDER BOB (3YR BAY GELDING)

TRAINER:	**David Barron**
FORM:	**3 -**
PEDIGREE:	**Big Bad Bob – Semiquaver (Mark Of Esteem)**
BHA RATING:	**—**
OPTIMUM TRIP:	**1m 2f +**

Looked an out-and-out stayer when a closing third on his debut in a 1m 1f maiden at Redcar last October, behind for much of the race until making headway in the straight despite being stopped in his run three furlongs from home.

Fourth foal and a half-brother to the talented but quirky Harwoods Volante and sprint winner Heartsong. Dam unraced full sister to 1m 5f winner Cinquilla out of a winner over middle distances.

Everything about this gelding points to his requiring a distance of ground. Trainer adept at bringing horses of this type along, and must be noted for staying handicaps once he acquires a mark.

FLEETFOOT JACK (3YR BAY COLT)

TRAINER:	**David O'Meara**
FORM:	**404 -**
PEDIGREE:	**Kyllachy – Move (Observatory)**
BHA RATING:	**67**
OPTIMUM TRIP:	**6f +**

One of the most interesting horses in this section, having shaped particularly well on the first and third of his three starts last season.

Outpaced and stayed on steadily on his debut in a 7f maiden at Redcar in September, making late headway alone on the nearside and running a similar race over the same course and distance in November, again doing his best work very late in the day.

Cost 185,000gns as a yearling, a second foal and a half-brother to a Listed-placed performer over a mile and a quarter. Dam, a winner over a mile, is a half-sister to French 1m 3f Listed winner Penchee from a middle-distance family.

Mixed messages regarding his likely optimum trip from his pedigree, but looked to need at least a mile last season so may take more from the dam's family than the sire.

Has shaped very well and is one to follow off what may turn out to be a reasonable mark.

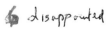 disappointed

KRUGER PARK (3YR BROWN COLT)

TRAINER:	Richard Fahey
FORM:	01 -
PEDIGREE:	Requinto – Definite Opinion (Kheleyf)
BHA RATING:	—
OPTIMUM TRIP:	6f

Has shown rather more than others in this section, but makes great appeal as the type of progressive sprinter who could be pitching into Pattern-class races by the autumn.

Was very green when fancied to go close on his debut at Pontefract in July, keeping on steadily at the finish, before showing the benefit of that experience when coming home strongly to beat the 78-rated Her Terms over an extended five furlongs in a maiden race at York.

Second foal of a 6f winning half-sister to a useful sprinter in Italy from the family of Group 3 winner Invincible Ash.

Probably favourably treated on 79 and has the class to win a competitive sprint handicap before progressing to better things.

MAKKADANGDANG (3YR ROAN GELDING)

TRAINER:	Andrew Balding
FORM:	002 -
PEDIGREE:	Mastercraftsman – Penny Cross (Efisio)
BHA RATING:	74
OPTIMUM TRIP:	1m +

Probably nothing out of the ordinary but showed enough to suggest races may come his way on the third of his three starts when staying on into second behind Mister Manduro in a 1m maiden auction race at Chelmsford in October. Might have been a length or two closer but for being switched for a clear run early in the straight.

Eighth foal and a half-brother to 2m hurdle winner Prompter and 2m 4f hurdle winner Quinsman.

Bred to be suited by a significant step up in trip and expected to be at his most effective over distances in excess of a mile and a half.

MAN OF VERVE (3YR BAY GELDING)

TRAINER:	**John Quinn**
FORM:	**031 -**
PEDIGREE:	**Dandy Man – She's Our Rock (Rock Of Gibraltar)**
BHA RATING:	**77**
OPTIMUM TRIP:	**1m**

Looks potentially useful in the context of his grade, having shaped well when third on his second start in a 5f maiden at Beverley before displaying a gritty attitude to get the better of the 75-rated Rag Tatter, the pair well clear of the third, in a 6f maiden auction contest on soft ground at Catterick.

Full brother to a winner over just short of a mile and looks very well bought at €15,000 as a two-year-old.

No reason why he should not stay a mile and has the size and scope to improve. Trainer has a good record with horses of this type.

MELINOE (3YR BAY FILLY)

TRAINER:	**Sir Mark Prescott**
FORM:	**0 -**
PEDIGREE:	**Sea The Stars – Persefona (Montjeu)**
BHA RATING:	—
OPTIMUM TRIP:	**1m 4f**

Caught the eye in a 7f maiden at Kempton on her sole start last season, hopelessly tailed off for much of the race until making headway to join the tail-end of the field turning for home. Steadily picked up ground thereafter to pass a handful of rivals inside the final furlong, finishing a full-of-running seventh of 12.

Cost 120,000gns as a yearling, having fetched 160,000gns as a foal. Third foal of a German 1m 3f winning half-sister to Group 2 middle-distance winner Sea Of Heartbreak from the family of Irish 1,000 Guineas and Yorkshire Oaks winner Sarah Siddons.

Bred to relish a mile and a half and showed more than enough on her debut to suggest she will win races, probably once she is handicapped.

May prove more than useful.

MOUNT ROCK (3YR BAY GELDING)

TRAINER:	**Michael Easterby**
FORM:	**4 -**
PEDIGREE:	**Mount Nelson – Holamo (Montjeu)**
BHA RATING:	—
OPTIMUM TRIP:	**1m 2f +**

Showed enough on his sole start last season to suggest he can win a maiden, shaping very well to finish fourth of 11 to

Mick Easterby – still as canny as ever

Brittanic in a slowly-run 7f maiden at Newcastle in December. Raced just off the pace and kept on well despite being short of room two furlongs from home.

Third foal of a half-sister to useful milers in the States.

Interesting to see whether connections opt for the handicap route or try to win a maiden. Whatever the case races should come his way.

SPRUCE LODGE (3YR BAY GELDING)

TRAINER:	**David Barron**
FORM:	**00 -**
PEDIGREE:	**Compton Place – Beautiful Lady (Peintre Celebre)**
BHA RATING:	**—**
OPTIMUM TRIP:	**1m**

Very promising on the evidence of his debut effort at Beverley, catching the eye with a strong-finishing sixth of 12 in a 5f maiden before running less well, having drifted right at the start, in a 6f maiden at Ripon.

Fourth foal and a half-brother to Outback Blue, a winner at up to a mile, and a 1m winner in the States. Dam, a winner at 1m 4f, is a full sister to 2m winner Bukit Tinggi from the family of a winner at 2m 4f.

Pedigree incorporates a mix of speed and stamina, but didn't lack pace at two and may be best at trips up to a mile. Definitely has ability and looks one to note once he acquires a handicap mark.

STARSHELL (3YR BAY GELDING)

TRAINER:	**Sir Mark Prescott**
FORM:	**000 -**
PEDIGREE:	**Sea The Stars – Aquarelle Bleue (Sadler's Wells)**
BHA RATING:	**—**
OPTIMUM TRIP:	**1m 4f**

Has not displayed obvious promise to the eye, but given the trainer's long-established way of working this well-bred gelding is likely to win races once stepped up in trip.

Stayed on steadily after being outpaced on his debut in an extended 1m maiden at Wolverhampton in September. Ran less well next time at Newcastle before shaping a little better on his third start at Wolverhampton in October.

Fifth foal and a full brother to 1m 5f winner Taqdees out of a mare who was placed over middle distances in France from the family of 1m 4f winner Amerique.

Handicapper appears to have exercised his right not to award a rating until he has more evidence from which to work.

Probably the most interesting of his trainer's team of three-year-olds and bred to improve by leaps and bounds once asked to tackle a distance of ground.

STUBYTUESDAY (3YR BAY GELDING)

TRAINER:	**Michael Easterby**
FORM:	**000 -**
PEDIGREE:	**Dick Turpin – Just Dreams (Salse)**
BHA RATING:	**58**
OPTIMUM TRIP:	**1m 2f +**

Revealed sufficient ability in three runs last season to suggest he can win middle-distance handicaps from his current mark.

Ran a fair first race at Wetherby in May, finishing fifth of nine. Did not reappear until October, shuffled along throughout to finish sixth of 12 in a 6f maiden. Shaped in a similar manner just under a month later in a 7f maiden at Redcar, finishing eighth of 14.

Half-brother to five winners, all at seven furlongs or less, but dam is a full-sister to St Leger and Gold Cup winner Classic Cliché.

Trainer dab hand at placing horses of this type to optimum effect. Interesting and one to note when the money is down.

TAXMEIFYOUCAN (3YR BAY GELDING)

TRAINER:	**Keith Dalgleish**
FORM:	**200 -**
PEDIGREE:	**Beat Hollow – Accounting (Sillery)**
BHA RATING:	**65**
OPTIMUM TRIP:	**1m 4f**

Shaped well on his debut in heavy ground at Hamilton in September, plugging on under hands and heels riding to finish a closing second to Election Day over an extended mile.

Did not seem to progress from that in his next two runs, finishing down the field in 1m and 1m 1f maidens at Redcar.

Eighth foal and a half-brother to six winners over trips ranging from a mile to 1m 4f.

Hard to assess on the evidence to hand, but leaves the impression he will be seen to greater effect over middle distances or more. Seemed to act well on easy ground.

TRADING POINT (3YR BAY COLT)

TRAINER:	**John Quinn**
FORM:	**21 -**
PEDIGREE:	**Siyouni – Zita Blues (Zieten)**
BHA RATING:	**81**
OPTIMUM TRIP:	**1m**

One of the most promising horses in this section.

Clear signs of promise when second on his debut in a 7f maiden at Ayr in September, keeping on strongly at the finish, before making all to win a 1m maiden at Haydock, lengthening in pleasing style to hold the late challenge of Materialist.

Half-brother to eight winners both on the Flat and over jumps, including 2m 1f hurdle winner Zitane and 1m 4f winner Salsablues.

Has great physical scope and should prove capable of performing creditably to a decent level. Stayed the mile well at Haydock and may get further.

WINE LIST (3YR CHESTNUT GELDING)

TRAINER:	**Andrew Balding**
FORM:	**0 -**
PEDIGREE:	**Champs Elysees – Masandra (Desert Prince)**
BHA RATING:	**—**
OPTIMUM TRIP:	**1m 2f +**

Looks sure to win races on the evidence of his highly promising debut in a 1m maiden at Newbury in October.

Left about five lengths when the stalls opened, made up the lost ground effortlessly on the nearside of the group to hold every chance approaching the final quarter mile before lack of peak fitness took its toll. Still managed to keep on well to finish sixth of 14, beaten just under seven lengths.

Fifth foal and a half-brother to Listed winner Elbereth and all-weather winner Masaadr, both over a mile and a half. Dam a half-sister to useful 1m 2f winner Masani from the family of French Poule d'Essai des Pouliches winner Masarika.

Bred to stay beyond a mile and has the potential to prove more than useful.

Very interesting.

THE DARK HORSES

The following horses, mostly unraced or lightly raced, have shaped with sufficient promise either at home or on the track to warrant respect when they appear.

ABJAR (3YR BAY COLT)

TRAINER:	Sir Michael Stoute
FORM:	Unraced
PEDIGREE:	Nathaniel – Kinnaird (Dr Devious)
BHA RATING:	—
OPTIMUM TRIP:	1m 2f +

Half-brother to useful stayer Berkshire, the progressive Abdon and 1m 4f winner Keenes Royale. Seventh foal of May Hill Stakes and Prix de l'Opera winner Kinnaird.

No shortage of stamina in his pedigree and looks one to keep in mind for middle distances. Has shown ability at home.

ACHIBUENO (3YR BAY COLT)

TRAINER:	Alain De Royer-Dupre
FORM:	Unraced
PEDIGREE:	Dansili – Altamira (Peintre Celebre)
RATING:	—
OPTIMUM TRIP:	1m 2f +

Half-brother to four winners out of a mare that won up to 1m 3f and is a full sister to 1m 2f Listed winner Andromeda Galaxy.

Bred to stay very well and apparently thought to have the class to prove competitive at a high level.

ADAMANT (3YR GREY COLT)

TRAINER:	**Sir Michael Stoute**
FORM:	**41 -**
PEDIGREE:	**Dalakhani – Attima (Zafonic)**
BHA RATING:	**81**
OPTIMUM TRIP:	**1m 2f +**

Showed the benefit of a considerate introduction when making all to win over an extended mile at Windsor in October.

Required plenty of stoking along, ridden prominently from the outset and shuffled along before pulling away well inside the final furlong.

Fifth foal and a full brother to French middle-distance winner Ottima out of a US Grade 2 winner over 1m 1f.

Quite a big sort, with the scope to improve beyond his mark and should stay a mile and a quarter.

AL GALAYEL (3YR BAY COLT)

TRAINER:	**Luca Cumani**
FORM:	**Unraced**
PEDIGREE:	**Zoffany – Glympse (Spectrum)**
BHA RATING:	**—**
OPTIMUM TRIP:	**1m 2f +**

Seventh foal and a half-brother to a handful of winners at trips ranging from five furlongs to two miles over hurdles. Dam, a daughter of staying influence Spectrum, is out of a 6f Listed winner.

Showed his trainer a fair level of ability at home last season. Likely to be brought along quietly with a view to the longer term.

ALWAHSH (3YR BAY COLT)

TRAINER:	**William Haggas**
FORM:	**0 -**
PEDIGREE:	**Dubawi – Gile Na Greine (Galileo)**
BHA RATING:	—
OPTIMUM TRIP:	**1m 2f +**

Showed a little more promise than the form book implies when staying on very late in a slowly-run 7f maiden at Newbury in September.

Full brother to 1m 1f winner Mawjood out of a 1,000 Guineas third full sister to Group 3 winner and 1,000 Guineas second Cuis Ghaire and 1m 1f Group 3 winner Scintillula.

Appears to have inherited rather more stamina than speed. Probably ran a little below the trainer's expectations at Newbury and looks the sort to improve with time over a mile or more.

Zoffany – developing into a high-class stallion

ANYTHINGTODAY (3YR BAY COLT)

TRAINER:	**Hugo Palmer**
FORM:	**341 -**
PEDIGREE:	**Zoffany – Corking (Montjeu)**
BHA RATING:	**82**
OPTIMUM TRIP:	**1m 4f +**

Improved markedly to defy a high draw when powering away to win an extended 1m maiden at Wolverhampton in November, beating a subsequent winner by two and a half lengths.

Had shaped quite well in his previous two starts, finishing a never-nearer third of 12 on his debut at Salisbury and then fourth of 11 at Newcastle.

Third foal of a 2m 1f winning half-sister to Sobriety, a useful performer up to 1m 2f, and to Violet, dam of a US Grade 2 winner. Half-brother to an all-weather winner over 1m 4f.

Bred to thrive over a mile and a half and may prove well treated on his opening mark.

BARNEY ROY (3YR BAY COLT)

TRAINER:	**Richard Hannon**
FORM:	**1 -**
PEDIGREE:	**Excelebration – Alina (Galileo)**
BHA RATING:	**91**
OPTIMUM TRIP:	**1m 2f +**

Could prove very useful, having impressed when showing a bright turn of foot to win a 1m maiden at Haydock on his debut last September.

Form no more than fair – second beaten next time but third a subsequent winner – but could not have impressed more with the manner of his success. Jockey reported afterwards that the colt had worked very well earlier in the season before meeting with a setback that necessitated having time off.

First foal of daughter of Galileo from the family of smart sprinter Gordon Lord Byron.

Looked very useful at Haydock and could be even better stepped up to a mile and a quarter. Was bought by Godolphin after his victory.

CAPE BYRON (3YR CHESTNUT COLT)

TRAINER:	**Roger Varian**
FORM:	**21 -**
PEDIGREE:	**Shamardal – Reem Three (Mark Of Esteem)**
BHA RATING:	**90**
OPTIMUM TRIP:	**1m +**

May have been beaten by a useful colt when going down by a length to Utmost in a 7f maiden at Leicester in October, leading a furlong from home but unable to contain the winner in the closing stages.

Brought out again just eight days later and showed a turn of foot to win a 7f maiden at Newmarket, held up in midfield before closing two furlongs out and quickening smartly to beat Manchego by two and a half lengths.

Fifth foal and a half-brother to 1m 4f winner Naqshabban, 2m hurdle and 2m 5f chase winner Goohar and to the useful stayer Ajman Princess. Dam is a well-related winning half-sister to 1m Group 2 winner Afsare.

Did very well to win over seven furlongs in view of the stamina on his dam's side. Likely to be effective at trips beyond a mile and has the potential and constitution to progress to Pattern-class company.

COMANCHE MOON (3YR CHESTNUT GELDING)

TRAINER:	**Charlie Appleby**
FORM:	**Unraced**
PEDIGREE:	**Shamardal – Lorena Wood (Woodman)**
OPTIMUM TRIP:	**1m**

Sixth foal and a half-brother to 7f US dirt winner One And Done out of a 6f winning full sister to Compton Dragon, a winner up to 1m 4f.

Unraced and gelded last season, but showed plenty of pace on the home gallops and has more than enough ability to win races.

DESERT DREAM (3YR BAY COLT)

TRAINER:	**Sir Michael Stoute**
FORM:	**0 -**
PEDIGREE:	**Oasis Dream – Rosika (Sakhee)**
BHA RATING:	—
OPTIMUM TRIP:	**1m +**

Shaped better than his finishing position suggests on his debut in a 1m maiden at Haydock in October, steadily away and soon settled in arrears before making progress in the straight and then tiring inside the final furlong.

Third foal and a half-brother to 1m 4f winner Dubka out of a Listed-placed and middle-distance winning half-sister to 1m 4f Listed winner Rambling Rose, dam of top-class performer Notnowcato.

Not an obvious inclusion from this yard but has shown up well in work at home and appeals as a progressive sort for handicaps and beyond.

DESERT EXPLORER (3YR BAY GELDING)

TRAINER:	**Eve Johnson Houghton**
FORM:	**Unraced**
PEDIGREE:	**Henrythenavigator – Bee Eater (Green Desert)**
OPTIMUM TRIP:	**1m**

Caught the eye when noted at Tattersalls October Yearling Sales in 2015 as a stocky individual with a great depth of girth and the scope to progress.

Fifth foal of Listed-placed Bee Eater, winner of four of her six starts, from the family of top-class Marling and Marwell. Half-brother to fair performers Picking Up Pieces and Leafcutter, both winners.

Not seen out last season and gelded, but comes from an excellent family and could be the type to pop up at long odds. In very good hands.

Eve Johnson Houghton – an underrated trainer

DREAM CASTLE (3YR BAY COLT)

TRAINER:	**Saeed bin Suroor**
FORM:	**Unraced**
PEDIGREE:	**Frankel – Sand Vixen (Dubawi)**
OPTIMUM TRIP:	**1m +**

Second live foal of 5f Group 2 winning half-sister to Listed winner So Will I from the family of useful sprinter Bumpkin.

Showed useful ability on home gallops last season with the potential to take high rank. Useful.

DUBAI THUNDER (3YR BAY COLT)

TRAINER:	**Saeed bin Suroor**
FORM:	**Unraced**
PEDIGREE:	**Dubawi – Gonbarda (Lando)**
BHA RATING:	—
OPTIMUM TRIP:	**1m 2f +**

Sixth foal and a half-brother to five winners, notably top-class Group 1 winner Farhh and useful winner up to 1m 2f Racing History. Dam won Group 1 in Germany.

From a stout bottom line and bred to come into his own over middle distances. The type to mature with the passing of time.

ELDRITCH (3YR BAY COLT)

TRAINER:	**John Gosden**
FORM:	**1 -**
PEDIGREE:	**Dark Angel – Henties Bay (Cape Cross)**
BHA RATING:	**77**
OPTIMUM TRIP:	**1m 2f +**

Overcame a troubled passage in the closing stages to win a 1m maiden at Haydock in October, shuffled along in the straight and having to be switched to get a clear run approaching the final furlong. Quickened impressively once clear.

Form of the race probably only moderate – close third now rated 67 – but the winner's turn of foot was impressive.

Fourth foal half-brother to Sparring, a winner up to 1m 4f, and 1m winner Wandsworth. Dam unraced half-sister to Middle Park winner Zieten and Cheveley Park Stakes winner Blue Duster.

Pedigree not devoid of speed but stayed the mile well at Haydock. Must have every chance from what may prove to be a favourable opening handicap mark.

ELUCIDATION (3YR BAY COLT)

TRAINER:	**Sir Michael Stoute**
FORM:	**31 -**
PEDIGREE:	**Oasis Dream – Mimalia (Silver Hawk)**
BHA RATING:	**88**
OPTIMUM TRIP:	**1m 2f +**

Shaped well when third of ten on his debut at Newmarket in August. Confirmed that promise the following month when making all to win a 7f maiden at Leicester by one and three-quarter lengths from Sporting Times.

Eighth foal and a half-brother to useful performers including Listed winner Unnefer and 1m 4f winner Peloponnese. Dam closely related to Derby winner Kris Kin.

Will probably prove superior to his current rating, especially when stepped up in trip.

EMINENT (3YR BAY COLT)

TRAINER:	**Martyn Meade**
FORM:	**1 -**
PEDIGREE:	**Frankel – You'll Be Mine (Kingmambo)**
BHA RATING:	**87**
OPTIMUM TRIP:	**1m +**

Not unfancied following useful work at home when making a winning debut in a 1m maiden at Newmarket in September. Settled in mid-division on the outside of the field before making steady headway and pulling clear inside the final furlong.

Form probably only ordinary by the standards of the track, but won with something in hand despite the concerns of connections about the good to firm ground.

Second foal and a half-brother to 6f winner As Good As Gold. Dam, third in the Group 1 Fillies' Mile, a half-sister to 1m 2f Group 1 winner Diamondsandrubies from the family of Quarter Moon, winner of the Group 1 Moyglare Stud Stakes and runner-up in the Oaks and Irish Oaks.

Could be the type to run well at long odds in Group-class company.

ERDOGAN (3YR BAY COLT)

TRAINER:	John Gosden
FORM:	Unraced
PEDIGREE:	Frankel – Dar Re Mi (Singspiel)
BHA RATING:	—
OPTIMUM TRIP:	1m 2f +

Cost 750,000gns as a yearling, the third foal of triple Group 1 winner Dar Re Mi, and a half-brother to Group 3 winner So Mi Dar.

Has shown enough to suggest he may live up to his high-class pedigree.

GOYA GIRL (3YR BAY FILLY)

TRAINER:	Ralph Beckett
FORM:	1 -
PEDIGREE:	Paco Boy – First Exhibit (Machiavellian)
BHA RATING:	—
OPTIMUM TRIP:	1m +

Made a winning debut in a 7f maiden fillies' contest at Wolverhampton in August, looking held two furlongs from home before knuckling down well to stay on strongly and win comfortably by a length from Suffragette City.

Form no more than moderate – runner-up ended the season a 12-race maiden rated on 61 – but much to like about the way the filly responded to her rider's urgings.

Sixth foal and a half-sister to four winners including Prime Exhibit and Figment. Dam unraced half-sister to 1m 4f Listed winner out of Prix Vermeille and Yorkshire Oaks winner My Emma.

Warrants a mark in the low 70s on the form shown at Wolverhampton. Trainer does well with fillies of this type, so watch for improvement through the season.

GUSTAVO FRING (3YR BAY COLT)

TRAINER:	**Richard Spencer**
FORM:	**Unraced**
PEDIGREE:	**Kodiac – Maleha (Cape Cross)**
OPTIMUM TRIP:	**7f +**

From an extremely low-profile yard, but showed ability at home and could pop up at a good price in a maiden or when handicapped.

Third foal of an unraced daughter of Cape Cross from the family of 1m Listed winner Yamal and 1m 2f Group 2 winner Faithful Son. Half-brother to winners Malilla and Desert Ranger.

Has plenty of speed in his pedigree and one to note for market interest at some point.

LAHORE (3YR BAY COLT)

TRAINER:	**Roger Varian**
FORM:	**Unraced**
PEDIGREE:	**Elusive Quality – Nayarra (Cape Cross)**
BHA RATING:	—
OPTIMUM TRIP:	**1m +**

First foal of an Italian Group 1 winning half-sister to useful performers at up to seven furlongs, from the family of top-class performer and sire Invincible Spirit and Prix de Diane winner Rafha.

Showed plenty of ability at home last season but was given time to mature. Could prove very useful.

MEDAHIM (3YR BAY COLT)

TRAINER:	**Richard Hannon**
FORM:	**1 -**
PEDIGREE:	**Kodiac – Novel Fun (Noverre)**
BHA RATING:	—
OPTIMUM TRIP:	**1m +**

Revealed a useful turn of foot to land a 6f maiden at Kempton in December. Steadily away and shuffled along on the turn for home, quickly made up ground on the leaders to win going away by three and a quarter lengths.

Cost 360,000gns as a yearling and the third foal of an unraced half-sister to three sprinters including 6f Group 3 winner Hunan.

Subsequent form of his race does not excite but could not have been more impressive and is highly regarded. Has abundant speed in his pedigree so may be best at trips up to a mile.

NAJASHEE (3YR GREY COLT)

TRAINER:	**Owen Burrows**
FORM:	**Unraced**
PEDIGREE:	**Invincible Spirit – Tonnara (Linamix)**
BHA RATING:	—
OPTIMUM TRIP:	**1m +**

Has shown up very well in work at home, both last season and this spring.

Sixth foal and a three-parts brother to 1m Group 1 winner Most Improved and a half-brother to 1m 4f Group 1 winner Ectot. Dam lightly-raced half-sister to a Group 3 winner over an extended ten furlongs.

Bred to stay beyond a mile on the dam's side, but shows plenty of pace at home and expected to be useful at least.

OMEROS (3YR CHESTNUT COLT)

TRAINER:	**Hugo Palmer**
FORM:	1 -
PEDIGREE:	**Poet's Voice – Caribbean Pearl (Silver Hawk)**
BHA RATING:	—
OPTIMUM TRIP:	**1m 2f +**

Steadied start when winning a 1m maiden at Chelmsford in October, bustled along in mid-division until powering through a gap on the rails to beat the strong-finishing Sufi by three-quarters of a length.

Fifth living foal out of a middle-distance winning daughter of Silver Hawk from the family of top-class filly Dabaweyaa.

Subsequent form of the race puts the winner on a mark in the low 80s, which could prove workable especially when he is stepped up in trip.

PERCY B SHELLEY (3YR CHESTNUT COLT)

TRAINER:	**John Gosden**
FORM:	**0 -**
PEDIGREE:	**Archipenko – Oshiponga (Barathea)**
BHA RATING:	**0 -**
OPTIMUM TRIP:	**1m 2f +**

Ridden very much with an eye to the future in an extended 1m 1f maiden at Wolverhampton in December. Last away and in arrears until the home turn, made steady headway thereafter and switched inside the final furlong to finish strongly up the rails. Appeared to have more to offer as he passed the post.

Winner rated 72, putting this performance on a mark in the high 60s.

Half-brother to seven winners over a variety of distances, ranging from five furlongs to 1m 5f. Dam, a winner over nine furlongs, is closely related to 1m 2f Grade 1 winner Miss Keller.

Looks destined for middle-distance handicaps. One to keep a close eye on.

PETERPORT (3YR BAY COLT)

TRAINER:	**John Gosden**
FORM:	**Unraced**
PEDIGREE:	**Nathaniel – Spinning Queen (Spinning World)**
BHA RATING:	**—**
OPTIMUM TRIP:	**1m +**

From a lovely family, closely related to Listed middle-distance winner Gallipot and half-brother to four other winners including Peterhof, Trade Commissioner and The Third Man. Dam made all to win the Group 1 Sun Chariot Stakes over a mile, beating Soviet Song by nine lengths with hugely talented Alexander Goldrun back in third.

Likely to be best over a mile or thereabouts.

Nathaniel – has yet to prove himself as a sire

PETITIONER (3YR BAY COLT)

TRAINER:	**Roger Charlton**
FORM:	**Unraced**
PEDIGREE:	**Dansili – Reflective (Seeking The Gold)**
BHA RATING:	—
OPTIMUM TRIP:	**1m 2f**

Fourth foal half-brother to Biographer, a winner at up to 1m 6f, out of an unraced three-parts sister to multiple Group 1 winner Hector Protector, 1,000 Guineas and Champion Stakes winner Bosra Sham and French Poule d'Essai des Poulains winner Shanghai.

Bred in the purple and should appreciate trips in excess of a mile.

Roger Charlton – the master of Beckhampton

SUNRIZE (3YR BAY COLT)

TRAINER:	**David O'Meara**
FORM:	**Unraced**
PEDIGREE:	**Azamour – Valmari (Kalanisi)**
BHA RATING:	—
OPTIMUM TRIP:	**1m 2f +**

First foal of a mare from the family of useful dual-purpose performer Minsk, out of a half-sister to Italian Derby winner White Muzzle.

Stoutly bred on both sides of his pedigree but shapes well at home and one to keep in mind for staying handicaps in the autumn.

THE GRAND VISIR (3YR BAY COLT)

TRAINER:	**William Haggas**
FORM:	**Unraced**
PEDIGREE:	**Frankel – Piping (Montjeu)**
BHA RATING:	—
OPTIMUM TRIP:	**1m 2f +**

Third foal half-brother to French 1m 3f winner Phedre out of unraced mare from the family of Almighty, a winner up to 1m 3f, and a half-sister to Arc winner Sagamix.

No shortage of stamina on the bottom line of his pedigree so should stay a mile and a quarter or more.

Frankel – will his progeny train on?

TIME ZONE (3YR BAY COLT)

TRAINER:	**Peter Chapple-Hyam**
FORM:	**1 -**
PEDIGREE:	**Kheleyf – Be Joyful (Teofilo)**
BHA RATING:	**82**
OPTIMUM TRIP:	**1m +**

Impressed with the manner of his maiden victory at Newmarket in September, travelling smoothly behind the leaders until bursting through a furlong out and holding on bravely to beat Doctor Bartolo, despite changing his legs once clear.

First foal of an unraced half-sister to a 1m Listed winner from the family of Cheveley Park Stakes winner Serious Attitude.

Subsequent form of those behind him suggests a mark of 82 is right but this may undervalue his ability. Sure to be well placed by his astute handler.

TOWIE (3YR BAY COLT)

TRAINER:	**Hughie Morrison**
FORM:	**Unraced**
PEDIGREE:	**Sea The Stars – Epping (Charnwood Forest)**
BHA RATING:	**—**
OPTIMUM TRIP:	**1m 2f +**

Ninth foal and a full brother to three winners including St Leger runner-up The Last Drop and 2m winner Ardlui. Dam, a winner over seven furlongs, is from the family of top-class Group 1 winner Sarah Siddons.

Showed ability at home last season despite being bred to stay well. Trainer adept at bringing horses of this type along quietly. One to note for later in the season.

UTMOST (3YR CHESTNUT COLT)

TRAINER:	**John Gosden**
FORM:	**1 -**
PEDIGREE:	**Giant's Causeway – Fugitive Angel (Alphabet Soup)**
BHA RATING:	**91**
OPTIMUM TRIP:	**1m +**

Won what time may show was an above-average maiden at Leicester in October, responding bravely to persistent urging to beat the useful Cape Byron, a good winner at Newmarket a few days later, by a length with Makkaar, also a winner next time out, beaten three and a quarter lengths in third.

First foal of a US Grade 3 turf winner from a good family of milers in the States.

Showed a plucky attitude to win this race and has the ability to prove effective at a decent level.

WEEKENDER (3YR BAY COLT)

TRAINER:	**John Gosden**
FORM:	**4 -**
PEDIGREE:	**Frankel – Very Good News (Empire Maker)**
BHA RATING:	—
OPTIMUM TRIP:	**1m +**

Well-supported in the market to even money to win a 1m maiden at Haydock in October but finished only fourth after being slowly away and then one-paced in the closing stages.

Comes from an exceptional family, the second foal of an unraced half-sister to Group 1 winners Banks Hill, Intercontinental, Cacique, Champs Elysees and Dansili.

Ran green through the race and evidently considered rather better than this form would suggest.

YAMARHABA MALAYEEN (3YR CHESTNUT COLT)

TRAINER:	**Simon Crisford**
FORM:	**Unraced**
PEDIGREE:	**Rip Van Winkle – Obama Rule (Danehill Dancer)**
BHA RATING:	—
OPTIMUM TRIP:	**1m +**

Second foal of a mare who won a Group 3 at nine furlongs and a full sister to Osaila, a winner at up to a mile, from the family of

Simon Crisford – has made a good start to his new career

Arc winner Detroit.

Bred along miling lines but entry for Derby suggests there is a belief that he will stay middle distances.

Shaped nicely at home last season and will be well placed by his promising handler.

YOUMKIN (3YR CHESTNUT COLT)

TRAINER:	**Saeed bin Suroor**
FORM:	**1 -**
PEDIGREE:	**Street Cry – Aryaamm (Galileo)**
BHA RATING:	—
OPTIMUM TRIP:	**1m 2f +**

Won what may turn out to have been a fair maiden at Nottingham in October, coming with a steady run on the outside of the field to beat Face The Facts, with subsequent winner Itsakindamagic in third.

Lengthened well given the slow pace of the race and was comfortably on top at the finish.

Seventh foal and a full brother to two winners, including the talented but ultimately disappointing Saamidd, and half-brother to 1m 2f winner Yarroom and 1m 4f Listed winner Talmada. Dam comes from the family of Barathea and Gossamer.

Hard to assess his level of form at this stage, but showed all the right signs in a race not entirely run to suit him. Probably more than useful.

THE IRISH DARK HORSES

The following Irish-trained horses, mostly unraced or lightly raced, have shaped with sufficient promise either at home or on the track to warrant respect when they appear.

ACT OF VALOUR (3YR BAY COLT)

TRAINER:	**Michael O'Callaghan**
FORM:	**0 -**
PEDIGREE:	**Harbour Watch – B Berry Brandy (Event Of The Year)**
TURF CLUB RATING:	—
OPTIMUM TRIP:	**1m 2f +**

Took a long time for the penny to drop on his sole outing last season, but eventually picked up nicely to finish fifth of ten to Perfect Storm in a 1m maiden at Navan in October.

Sixth foal and a half-brother to three winners out of a half-sister to Group 2 winner Strong Suit.

Unlikely to be top class but could be the type to run well at long odds in an early maiden.

AIR SUPREMACY (3YR BAY COLT)

TRAINER:	**Aidan O'Brien**
FORM:	**Unraced**
PEDIGREE:	**Galileo – Crystal Valkyrie (Danehill)**
OPTIMUM TRIP:	**1m 2f +**

Not cheap at 600,000gns as a yearling and a full brother to Granddukeoftuscany, a lightly-raced winner of an extended 1m 4f maiden, and Rasmiya, also lightly raced and a winner over an extended 11 furlongs at Bath. Half-brother to four other winners including 7f Group 3 winner Sent From Heaven.

Has shown something at home and expected to come into his own over middle distances.

Aidan O'Brien – irrepressible at the highest level

ALDHARA (3YR BAY FILLY)

TRAINER:	**Dermot Weld**
FORM:	**Unraced**
PEDIGREE:	**Dubawi – Bethrah (Marju)**
OPTIMUM TRIP:	**1m 2f +**

Third foal of Irish 1,000 Guineas winner from the family of Reve D'Oscar and French 1m 3f Group 3 winner and useful hurdler Numide.

Shaped in encouraging fashion at home last season and expected to prove one of the better three-year-old fillies in her powerful yard.

AMBASSADORIAL (3YR BAY COLT)

TRAINER:	**Michael Halford**
FORM:	**11 -**
PEDIGREE:	**Elusive Quality – Tactfully (Discreet Cat)**
TURF CLUB RATING:	—
OPTIMUM TRIP:	**1m +**

Won both his starts in a similar manner, steadily away from the stalls and off the pace turning for home before coming with a steady run on the outside to lead a furlong out and pull clear.

Beat fair performer Executive Force in a 7f Listed contest on the second occasion.

First foal of a 1m winning half-sister to a sprint winning daughter of Discreet Cat.

Has a very relaxed way of racing and should prove effective at Group level. Runs as if he should stay a mile and bred to do so.

Michael Halford – sure to get the best out of Ambassadorial

AMUSE BOUCHE (3YR CHESTNUT COLT)

TRAINER:	**Dermot Weld**
FORM:	**Unraced**
PEDIGREE:	**Distorted Humor – Mousse Au Chocolat (Hennessy)**
OPTIMUM TRIP:	**1m**

Third foal of French Listed winner from the family of Listed-placed Ronans Bay.

Shaped quite nicely in preparatory work at home last season but given time to mature. Bred to suit a mile.

ANEEN (3YR BAY FILLY)

TRAINER:	**Kevin Prendergast**
FORM:	**41 -**
PEDIGREE:	**Lawman – Asheerah (Shamardal)**
TURF CLUB RATING:	—
OPTIMUM TRIP:	**1m +**

Shaped well when fourth of 18 on her debut in a 7f maiden at Leopardstown in September and showed the benefit when quickening impressively to beat 24 rivals in a 7f maiden at the Curragh a month later. Form reads well with the third, beaten almost five lengths, now rated on 84.

Second foal and a half-sister to Irish 2,000 Guineas winner Awtaad out of a Listed-placed half-sister to Group-placed two-year-old winners Aaraas and Alshahbaa.

Comes from an excellent family and already has the look of a Group-class performer.

ASMAT (3YR BAY FILLY)

TRAINER:	**Dermot Weld**
FORM:	**Unraced**
PEDIGREE:	**Dansili – Askeria (Sadler's Wells)**
OPTIMUM TRIP:	**1m 4f**

Third foal and a half-sister to winner Ashraf out of a dam closely related to top-class middle-distance performer Azamour.

Comes from a high-class family but has shown pace in her work at home, so may prove effective at around a mile. Well regarded by her trainer.

ASSONANCE (3YR BAY FILLY)

TRAINER:	Joseph O'Brien
FORM:	Unraced
PEDIGREE:	Fastnet Rock – Social Honour (Entrepreneur)
OPTIMUM TRIP:	1m +

Second foal and a half-sister to 6f to 1m winner Tones out of an Italian winner from 5f to 1m, herself a half-sister to five winners from the family of US Grade 1 performer Windy's Daughter.

Shaped nicely in her work at home last season and expected to prove effective at around a mile.

AURORA BUTTERFLY (3YR GREY FILLY)

TRAINER:	Willie McCreery
FORM:	Unraced
PEDIGREE:	Born To Sea – Daimonaka (Akarad)
OPTIMUM TRIP:	1m 2f

A half-sister to nine winners including Group 3 winner and French Guineas runner-up Diamond Green, Group 2 winner Diamilina and Group 3 winner Diamonixa. The dam is a half-sister to Group winners including Diamond Mix and Diamond Dance.

From a prolific family and has shown enough at home to raise hopes she may follow suit.

CALGATH (3YR BAY COLT)

TRAINER:	**Tracey Collins**
FORM:	**0 -**
PEDIGREE:	**Fastnet Rock – Minor Vamp (Hawk Wing)**
TURF CLUB RATING:	—
OPTIMUM TRIP:	**1m +**

Considered much better than he showed when finishing last of eight on his sole start last season.

Second foal of a Group-placed half-sister to 6f winner Play Misty For Me and a useful winner up to 1m 2f.

One to note for a big-priced win, possibly when handicapped.

CLIFFS OF MOHER (3YR BAY COLT)

TRAINER:	**Aidan O'Brien**
FORM:	**01 -**
PEDIGREE:	**Galileo – Wave (Dansili)**
TURF CLUB RATING:	—
OPTIMUM TRIP:	**1m 4f**

Showed promise when staying on well into fifth in a 7f maiden at Cork in October before powering away to win a similar event a fortnight later at Leopardstown.

First foal of a 5f winner at two, related to Listed winner Look At Me and Francis Of Assisi, from the family of Henrythenavigator.

Did well to win over seven furlongs given the stamina in his pedigree. Rated highly enough to become a possible contender in the Classics, probably at his most effective stepped up beyond a mile.

DRUIDS CROSS (3YR BAY COLT)

TRAINER:	Joseph O'Brien
FORM:	001 -
PEDIGREE:	Cape Cross – Shell Garland (Sadler's Wells)
TURF CLUB RATING:	90
OPTIMUM TRIP:	1m 2f +

Definitely not straightforward, having tried to hang right when coming with a winning run to land a 7f maiden at Dundalk in November, but no doubting his ability.

Beat the 81-rated Rock In Peace, a dual winner since, pulling away near the finish once his stamina kicked in. Had shown little on his first two starts.

Sixth foal and a half-brother to Sands Of Fortune, a winner on the Flat over 2m 5f, and 1m 4f winner Kris Kin Line. Dam from the family of 1m 6f listed winner Yeoman's Point.

Bred to stay middle distances at least and may be one for a staying handicap, perhaps towards the back-end of the season.

Joseph O'Brien – gradually finding his feet as a trainer

DUBAI SAND (3YR CHESTNUT COLT)

TRAINER:	Jim Bolger
FORM:	021 -
PEDIGREE:	Teofilo – Bring Back Matron (Rock Of Gibraltar)
TURF CLUB RATING:	104
OPTIMUM TRIP:	1m 2f

Looked gutsy when battling on well under a prominent ride to win a 1m 1f Listed contest at Leopardstown in October having shaped well earlier in the month when second of 14 at the Curragh.

Fourth foal and a half-brother to useful performer Vocaliser and 1m 2f winner Miracle Cure. Dam, a maiden, from the family of Listed winners Graduated and Speirbhean.

Stayed the nine furlongs well at Leopardstown but not sure to get much further. Will be suited to good ground and expected to take his chance in an early trial.

ENDLESS ENDEAVOUR (3YR BAY GELDING)

TRAINER:	John Joseph Murphy
FORM:	000 -
PEDIGREE:	Sir Percy – Ryella (Cozzene)
TURF CLUB RATING:	59
OPTIMUM TRIP:	1m 2f +

Very lowly rated on 59 having been beaten over 50 lengths in three starts at the Curragh, Limerick and Dundalk.

Sixth foal and a half-brother to three winners out of a well-related winner over six furlongs in Canada.

No obvious signs of ability on the track but shows more at home than his form on the track. One to note at a big price in a handicap.

ENEMY OF THE STATE (3YR BAY COLT)

TRAINER:	**Johnny Levins**
FORM:	**0 - 0**
PEDIGREE:	**Kodiac – Bacchanalia (Blues Traveller)**
TURF CLUB RATING:	**—**
OPTIMUM TRIP:	**1m +**

Not an obvious candidate for inclusion in this section, but showed he had ability in his first three starts, all at Dundalk.. Slowly away each time before running on in the closing stages, the first time over five furlongs and the next time over six, before stepping up to a mile.

Eighth foal and a half-brother to three winners at trips ranging from five furlongs to a mile.

Probably one for handicaps over a mile or more.

ERANA (3YR BAY FILLY)

TRAINER:	**Dermot Weld**
FORM:	**Unraced**
PEDIGREE:	**Siyouni – Erdiyna (Selkirk)**
OPTIMUM TRIP:	**1m 2f +**

Fourth foal of a winner up to 1m 4f from the family of Irish Oaks and French Leger winner Ebadiyla, Ascot Gold Cup winner Estimate and top-class Edabiya.

Comes from one of the Aga Khan's most successful families. Shaped nicely at home last season and bred to improve with time.

ESPOIR D'SOLEIL (3YR CHESTNUT FILLY)

TRAINER:	**Dermot Weld**
FORM:	**Unraced**
PEDIGREE:	**Galileo – Lady Luck (Kris)**
OPTIMUM TRIP:	**1m 2f +**

Ninth foal and a half-sister to seven winners including Group 1 Tattersalls Gold Cup winner Casual Conquest, 1m Group 3 winner Afternoon Sunlight, 7f Listed winner Elusive Double and others.

Bred along miling lines on the dam's side but sire's influence should enable her to stay further. Shapes nicely at home.

Dermot Weld – yet another strong team for 2017

EZIYRA (3YR CHESTNUT FILLY)

TRAINER:	**Dermot Weld**
FORM:	**2121 -**
PEDIGREE:	**Teofilo – Eytarna (Dubai Destination)**
TURF CLUB RATING:	**107**
OPTIMUM TRIP:	**1m +**

Tail flasher, but talented having won a 7f maiden at Galway in July and then running second to Sea Of Grace in a 1m Group 3 at the Curragh a month later.

Improved again on her final start, when hooded for the first time and beating Grecian Light by two lengths in the Group 3 C.L. and M.F. Weld Park Stakes, leading on the nearside a furlong from home and keeping on well despite flashing her tail.

Needs to improve, but trainer hopes she will prove good enough to compete at Classic level.

FAMOUS PEARL (3YR CHESTNUT FILLY)

TRAINER:	**John Oxx**
FORM:	**Unraced**
PEDIGREE:	**Way Of Light – Santa Christiana (Danehill Dancer)**
OPTIMUM TRIP:	**1m +**

Second foal of a maiden from the family of French 1m Listed winner Moon Is Up and Miesque.

Showed ability at home last season and bred to be effective at a mile. Expected to play a part in Pattern company.

FARADAYS LAW (3YR BAY FILLY)

TRAINER:	Willie McCreery
FORM:	0 -
PEDIGREE:	Lawman – Faraday Light (Rainbow Quest)
TURF CLUB RATING:	—
OPTIMUM TRIP:	1m 4f +

Shaped quite nicely when staying on to finish ninth of 25 in the 7f maiden at the Curragh won by Aneen in October.

Sixth foal and a full sister to Irish 1,000 Guineas winner Just The Judge and 1m winner Amber Silk. Dam, who showed nothing on the track, is a half-sister to 1m 4f Group 3 winner High Heeled.

Bred to stay well and could pop up at a good price somewhere.

GLASTONBURY SONG (3YR CHESTNUT COLT)

TRAINER:	Ger Lyons
FORM:	1 -
PEDIGREE:	Casamento – Nesmeh (More Than Ready)
TURF CLUB RATING:	—
OPTIMUM TRIP:	1m

One of the most impressive maiden winners seen in Ireland last season, coming from off the pace to quicken away to beat 13 rivals without coming under pressure at any stage.

Form of the race no more than moderate – runner-up rated 80 on the all-weather – but winner is highly regarded and could prove good enough for Pattern company.

Third foal and a half-brother to a couple of fair performers up to 1m 2f.

Promises to be useful.

GRANDEE (3YR BAY COLT)

TRAINER:	**Jessica Harrington**
FORM:	**0331 -**
PEDIGREE:	**Lope De Vega – Caravan Of Dreams (Anabaa)**
TURF CLUB RATING:	**97**
OPTIMUM TRIP:	**1m 2f +**

Beaten three times before coming with a steady run in the straight to beat subsequent winner Dubai Sand in a 1m 1f maiden at the Curragh in October. Won going away despite edging right once clear.

Full brother to Sabre Squadron and half-brother to 1m 6f Flat and hurdle winner Weather Watch. Dam from the family of 2m Group 3 winner Royal And Regal.

May be short of Group 1 class, but was progressing last autumn and trainer does well with horses of this type. May pop up at a good price early in the spring.

HARBOUR BEACON (3YR BAY COLT)

TRAINER:	**Ger Lyons**
FORM:	**22 -**
PEDIGREE:	**Harbour Watch – Blue Beacon (Fantastic Light)**
TURF CLUB RATING:	**—**
OPTIMUM TRIP:	**1m 2f +**

One of the better maidens in this section, second in two one-mile contests at Navan in October, travelling very smoothly on each occasion, and staying on well at the finish without doing quite enough to win.

Fifth foal and half-brother to Asian Wing, a winner up to two miles, and 7f winner Like No Other. Dam out of Cheveley Park Stakes winner Blue Duster.

Likely to improve significantly for a step up to a mile and looks a formality to win a maiden at least. Likeable sort.

HARRANA (3YR GREY FILLY)

TRAINER:	**Dermot Weld**
FORM:	**Unraced**
PEDIGREE:	**New Approach – Hazarafa (Daylami)**
OPTIMUM TRIP:	**1m 2f +**

Third foal half-sister to middle-distance winner Harasava out of a 1m 4f Listed winning half-sister to Derby winner Harzand and Group 3 winner Harasiya.

Extremely well related and bred to come into her own over middle distances later in the season.

HAZAMA (3YR BAY FILLY)

TRAINER:	**Dermot Weld**
FORM:	**Unraced**
PEDIGREE:	**Azamour – Haziyna (Halling)**
OPTIMUM TRIP:	**1m 2f +**

Second foal of a 1m 2f Group-placed half-sister to Derby winner Harzand, Group 3 winner Harasiya and 1m 4f Listed winner Hazarafa.

Bred along similar lines to the aforementioned Harrana but with a little more stamina in the pedigree. Shaped well at home.

LONGING (3YR BAY FILLY)

TRAINER:	**Aidan O'Brien**
FORM:	**Unraced**
PEDIGREE:	**Galileo – Like A Dame (Danehill)**
OPTIMUM TRIP:	**1m 4f**

Fifth foal and a full sister to the maiden Dewdrop and a half-sister to Group 3 winner Ladys First out of a winning daughter of 1m 4f Group 2 winner Animatrice.

Cost 1,000,000gns as a yearling. Shaped well at home and likely to prove at her most effective over middle distances.

Galileo – one of the great sires of our time

MODERN APPROACH (3YR BAY FILLY)

TRAINER:	Jim Bolger
FORM:	Unraced
PEDIGREE:	New Approach – Janey Muddles (Lawman)
OPTIMUM TRIP:	1m 4f

First foal of a 6f winning half-sister to My Single Malt, a winner up to an extended mile, from the family of Listed winner Misu Bond and 7f Group 3 winner Air Chief Marshal.

Showed fair ability at home last season given her dam's predisposition to stamina. An interesting prospect, especially for later in the season.

NATURALIST (3YR BAY COLT)

TRAINER:	William McCreery
FORM:	Unraced
PEDIGREE:	Nathaniel – Vassiana (Anabaa)
OPTIMUM TRIP:	1m 2f

Ninth foal and related to six winners including Group 3 winner Girouette and others, mainly up to a mile. Dam, a winner over a mile, is a full sister to a Group 3 sprint winner.

Shaped well in steady work at home and expected to win races, especially when stepped up to a mile and a half.

NEPTUNE (3YR CHESTNUT COLT)

TRAINER:	**Dermot Weld**
FORM:	**Unraced**
PEDIGREE:	**Galileo – Caumshinaun (Indian Ridge)**
TURF CLUB RATING:	**—**
OPTIMUM TRIP:	**1m +**

Extremely well-related full brother to Irish 1,000 Guineas winner Nightime, 2m winner Olympiad and 1m 4f winner Phaenomena.

Dam won at between six furlongs and a mile.

Bred to be more than useful.

ON ICE (3YR BAY FILLY)

TRAINER:	**Joseph O'Brien**
FORM:	**Unraced**
PEDIGREE:	**Galileo – Beltisaal (Belmez)**
OPTIMUM TRIP:	**1m 4f**

Stoutly bred 13th foal and a full sister to talented but ultimately disappointing Group 1 winner Kingsbarns, 1m 4f winner Egyptian Warrior and half-sister to seven winners including Group 3 winner Belle Artiste and US Grade 3 winner Sweeter Still.

Bred to thrive once she is asked to tackle a distance of ground.

PANSTARR (3YR BAY FILLY)

TRAINER:	**Jim Bolger**
FORM:	**Unraced**
PEDIGREE:	**Pivotal – Halle Bop (Dubai Millennium)**
OPTIMUM TRIP:	**1m**

Sixth foal and a half-sister to a winner over 7f. Dam, a 6f winner at two, is a half-sister to Group-placed winner Queen Of Naples from the family of Derby winner Oath.

No shortage of speed in her pedigree but entry for the Irish Oaks suggests she is deemed capable of staying middle distances.

RENAISSANCE MAN (3YR BAY COLT)

TRAINER:	**Joseph O'Brien**
FORM:	**Unraced**
PEDIGREE:	**Galileo – My Renee (Kris S)**
TURF CLUB RATING:	—
OPTIMUM TRIP:	**1m 2f +**

Seventh foal and a half-brother to five winners including 1m 4f Group 2 winner Banimpire and Listed-placed My Spirit. Dam, winner of a Listed race over 1m 4f, is from the family of Arc winner Detroit.

Has needed time but shows something at home.

SOLO SAXOPHONE (3YR BAY COLT)

TRAINER:	**Dermot Weld**
FORM:	**Unraced**
PEDIGREE:	**Frankel – Society Hostess (Seeking The Gold)**
OPTIMUM TRIP:	**1m**

Half-brother to Sailors Swan, Listed-placed over an extended five furlongs, out of a Grade 3 US winner over an extended six furlongs and a mile from the family of US dirt performer Twilight Agenda from the family of Refuse To Bend.

Bred for a mile but holds an entry for the Irish Derby, so expectations may be that he will stay further. Shapes nicely at home and expected to prove one of the yard's better performers.

STAY WITH ME (3YR GREY FILLY)

TRAINER:	**Darren Bunyan**
FORM:	**Unraced**
PEDIGREE:	**Cape Cross – Louverissa (Verglas)**
OPTIMUM TRIP:	**1m 2f +**

Fourth foal of a half-sister to Lulani, a winner up to 1m 1f, 7f winner Hermarna and Medicina, a winner up to 1m 2f. Dam an unraced half-sister to 2,000 Guineas and Irish 2,000 Guineas winner Cockney Rebel.

Could prove well bought at €25,000 as a yearling given the promise she showed at home last season. One to note for a long-priced success.

THE SWAGMAN (3YR CHESTNUT COLT)

TRAINER:	**Aidan O'Brien**
FORM:	**Unraced**
PEDIGREE:	**Galileo – Ventura (Spectrum)**
OPTIMUM TRIP:	**1m 4f**

Ninth foal and full brother to US 1m 6f winner Cedar Mountain and a half-brother to four winners including Moonlight Cloud. Dam, a winner over a mile, from the family of Generous.

Bred to be useful but unlikely to come into his own until he is asked to tackle a distance of ground.

TIME DEE (3YR GREY COLT)

TRAINER:	**Paul Deegan**
FORM:	**4 -**
PEDIGREE:	**Jukebox Jury – Tech Exceed (Exceed And Excel)**
TURF CLUB RATING:	**—**
OPTIMUM TRIP:	**1m 2f +**

Caught the eye when staying on steadily under considerate handling to finish a never-nearer fourth of 14 to First Premio in a 1m maiden at Dundalk in October.

Second foal of an Italian 1m 2f Group 3 winner from the family of Tiger Hill.

Has a fair amount of ability and may pop up at a good price for his low-profile trainer.

TITUS (3YR BAY COLT)

TRAINER:	**Dermot Weld**
FORM:	**1 -**
PEDIGREE:	**Dansili – Mirror Lake**
	(Dubai Destination)
TURF CLUB RATING:	—
OPTIMUM TRIP:	**1m 2f +**

Quietly impressive when beating 14 rivals in a 1m Leopardstown maiden in October, travelling comfortably in fourth before taking the lead early in the straight. Time of the race was modest but held on well from the strong-finishing Venice Beach.

Second foal and a half-brother to a 7f winner out of a 1m 2f Listed winning half-sister to Mirrored from the family of Group winners Danefair, Prove and Vortex.

Stayed the mile well at Leopardstown and rated quite highly by his trainer. Warrants a run in an early trial.

TOCCO D'AMORE (3YR BAY FILLY)

TRAINER:	**Dermot Weld**
FORM:	**Unraced**
PEDIGREE:	**Raven's Pass – Spirit Of Tara**
	(Sadler's Wells)
OPTIMUM TRIP:	**1m 2f +**

Twelfth foal and a half-sister to Group 2 winner Echo Of Light, 1m winner Irish History, 1m 4f winner Akarem, 1m 2f winner Flame Of Gibraltar and 1m 1f winner Multazem. Dam, a winner over 1m 4f, is a full-sister to top-class mare Salsabil.

Cost €2 million as a yearling and comes from one of the best families in the stud book.

WISCONSIN (3YR BAY COLT)

TRAINER:	**Aidan O'Brien**
FORM:	**Unraced**
PEDIGREE:	**Deep Impact – Peeping Fawn (Danehill)**
OPTIMUM TRIP:	**1m 2f +**

Fourth foal of four-times Group 1 and Irish Oaks winner Peeping Fawn from the family of French Group 1 winner Thewayyouare.

Half-brother to Sir John Hawkins, a winner over six furlongs at two, and middle-distance winner Purely Priceless.

Shaped nicely at home last season and can win over a mile before progressing over further.

Deep Impact – winner of seven Grade 1 races in Japan

WORLD STAGE (3YR BAY COLT)

TRAINER:	Aidan O'Brien
FORM:	Unraced
PEDIGREE:	Galileo – Penchant (Kyllachy)
OPTIMUM TRIP:	1m +

Half-brother to the top-class Garswood out of an unraced daughter of Kyllachy, from the family of Group 3 winner Infallible and Group-placed Watchable.

Entered for the Irish Derby but may be best suited to trips short of a mile and a half. Has shown something at home.

ZIHAAM (3YR CHESTNUT GELDING)

TRAINER:	Kevin Prendergast
FORM:	Unraced
PEDIGREE:	Dutch Art - Hymnsheet (Pivotal)
OPTIMUM TRIP:	7f

Third foal of a full sister to 1m 2f Group 1 winner Chorist, a daughter of Pivotal.

Shaped well in work last season but subsequently gelded. Has ability but may prove best suited to trips short of a mile.

THE QIPCO 2,000 GUINEAS PREVIEW

Churchill currently stands at the head of the market for the 2,000 Guineas, having displayed progressive form through the summer culminating in a workmanlike success in the Dewhurst Stakes.

His career started at the Curragh in May, when he stayed on steadily to finish third in a 6f maiden. There was plenty of talk about him before his next appearance in the Chesham Stakes at Royal Ascot, with reports that some close to the yard, even at that early stage, rated him their leading 2,000 Guineas contender. His victory there was achieved in a manner that would prove characteristic of the colt in his next four races, racing a little keenly and then requiring firm handling to assert his superiority inside the final furlong. Hanging left, he held on to win all out from subsequent winner Isomer, who ended the season on a mark of 99.

Churchill's next appearance came in the Group 3 Tyros Stakes at Leopardstown in July. Once again he was no more than workmanlike, looking in trouble two furlongs from home before hanging on dourly from Tommy Stack's Alexios Komnenos, a son of Choisir who ran well but was not seen out again.

It was a similar story a month later in the Group 2 Futurity Stakes before he stepped into Group 1 company for the first time in the National Stakes at the Curragh. A little keen in the early stages, he was short of room two furlongs from home as Mehmas leaned towards him, before responding to Ryan Moore's urgings to win going away by just over four lengths.

Churchill's final race of the season came in the Dewhurst Stakes, for which he started 8/11 to beat a field that included

Churchill – destined for greatness

Godolphin's Gimcrack Stakes winner and Group 1 Middle Park runner-up Blue Point, Champagne Stakes winner Rivet and John Gosden's promising dual winner Seven Heavens.

As before, Churchill raced keenly for the first two furlongs before having to be shuffled along to hold his place at halfway. Switched right two furlongs from home, he responded to pressure to beat stable companion Lancaster Bomber by one and a quarter lengths. The margin of superiority over the runner-up was less than in their last two meetings – he had been five and a half lengths and nine lengths ahead of him before – but Lancaster Bomber was probably improving as less than a month later he ran second in the Breeders' Cup Juvenile Turf.

Churchill is unlikely ever to impress in his races. He tends to get warm, race keenly and then battle it out rather than quicken. In six races he has never shown anything approaching a turn of foot. What he does do, though, is gallop and dig deep at the business end of the race. He may have covered 41 furlongs in his six starts, but to my eyes he has only raced for about five of them.

Churchill, a son of Galileo, runs as if he will not only stay but appreciate a step up to a mile. His pedigree, though, is not entirely emphatic in that respect. His dam, Meow, won a 5f listed race as a two-year-old – her only season to race – and is a daughter of Storm Cat and the speedy Airwave.

Aidan O'Brien concedes that the colt "doesn't do a lot, and never will", but adds that he has "tons up his sleeve and is the most imposing horse we have ever trained". He adds that the colt "relaxes and sleeps" and has a "very strong mind".

Ryan Moore expects Churchill to stay a mile and a quarter, while Aidan O'Brien says that he could get even further because he is so "economical as a galloper".

From the evidence to hand Churchill should relish the stiff Rowley Mile and it's easy to imagine him striding away inside the final furlong. He would be vulnerable to a rival with a turn of foot that has the class to stay with him, but he has great physical scope and handles all types of ground.

The only other horse in single figures for the 2,000 Guineas is Churchill's stable companion **Caravaggio**, who ended the season the unbeaten winner of four starts.

In contrast to the favourite, Caravaggio has both natural pace and a turn of foot. Starting with a very easy victory in a 5f maiden at Dundalk in April, he then won a Listed race over the same trip at the Curragh before justifying favouritism in the Coventry Stakes, powering up the middle of the track to beat Mehmas by two and a quarter lengths. His final appearance came in the Group 1 Phoenix Stakes in August, where he landed odds of 1/8 by four lengths from stable companion Courage Under Fire, who ended the season on a mark of 103.

Plans to run next in the Middle Park were shelved after Caravaggio pulled a muscle in his ribcage soon after the race. He did not race again.

The concern of connections about the soft ground in the

Caravaggio – will he stay the mile?

Coventry proved unfounded and he looked far more at home on the good to firm going at the Curragh in August. Aidan O'Brien has already gone on record about the colt's speed, although his pedigree gives some grounds for optimism regarding his staying a mile.

His sire, Scat Daddy, won up to nine furlongs in Grade 1 company while his dam has milers in her family. The trainer says he will run Caravaggio over seven furlongs in the spring before deciding on the Guineas. My view is that the colt will be tried over a mile at some point, although whether that happens at Newmarket in May could be governed by the state of the ground.

War Decree progressed from his first two runs to beat Thunder Snow by one and three-quarter lengths at Goodwood in July. It took him a few strides to pick up but he was coming away nicely inside the final furlong. The runner-up has since won a Group 1 at Saint-Cloud in October and in February landed the UAE 2,000 Guineas at Meydan.

Rivet, trained by William Haggas, is expected to take his chance in the Guineas.

Promising on his Ascot debut, when he ran on well to finish second in a 6f maiden, he then came away in the final furlong to win the Convivial Maiden Stakes at York over a furlong further. His next victory was a hard-fought head defeat of Thunder Snow in the Group 2 Champagne Stakes at Doncaster before going to Newmarket for the Dewhurst Stakes. Racing a little keenly off a modest pace, he plugged on at one pace to finish fifth of seven, three and a half lengths behind the winner. The trainer suggested afterwards that the colt didn't handle the dip.

Rivet returned to winning ways a fortnight later in the Group 1 Racing Post Trophy at Doncaster. Under an enterprising ride from Andrea Atzeni and despite this being his first attempt at a mile, he made all to beat Yucatan pulling away by one and three-quarter lengths.

Rivet is bred to appreciate further than a mile. A son of Fastnet Rock, his full brother won over nine furlongs and other siblings won over a mile and a quarter. His dam Starship, a daughter of Galileo, won over a mile.

It was a brave decision to make all the running on Rivet at his first attempt over a mile. The tactic certainly suited the colt, but the concern regarding the Guineas is the track. On the book, he has about 7lb to find with Churchill, but with proven Group 1 form over a mile to his name he warrants consideration.

Not much went right for Criquette Head-Maarek last season but a high spot came when **National Defense** made all the running to win the 1m Group 1 Prix Jean-Luc Lagardere on Arc weekend. The son of Invincible Spirit found a turn of foot from the front to beat Salouen by four and a half lengths, with

Ballydoyle colt Whitecliffsofdover a short neck back in third.

This was a step up from his previous run, when he finished third of six in a Group 3. The trainer said afterwards that the colt has "a lot of energy" and appreciated making the running.

Despite being by the sprinter Invincible Spirit there is every chance that National Defense will stay beyond a mile. His half-brother Cascading, by Teofilo, won at a mile and a half and the dam, who was unraced, is closely related to a mile and a quarter winner.

Plans for National Defense are uncertain, as I write, but as with Rivet this winner of a Group 1 over a mile is entitled to be in the line-up.

Thunder Snow has finished behind Caravaggio, War Decree, Rivet and Churchill on four separate occasions but then beat

Rivet – bred to stay beyond a mile

South Seas by five lengths in the Criterium International at Saint-Cloud before easily landing the UAE 2,000 Guineas. The son of Helmet has probably improved since last summer but he needs to if he is to reverse last summer's form with his old adversaries.

Godolphin have a less-exposed prospect named **Zorion**. The son of Smart Strike, who is trained by Jim Bolger, overcame signs of greenness to win at Roscommon on his sole start last August. He didn't seem to be going all that well turning for home, but by the line he was six and a half lengths clear of Joy For Mary. The runner-up is now rated a lowly 66, which puts the form into perspective, but Zorion looks just the tough sort of colt his trainer excels with. He should stay a mile.

Godolphin acquired a half-share in David Elsworth's **Swiss Storm** in February. The son of Frankel built on a promising debut at Haydock in September when beating ten rivals in a 7f maiden at Newbury just over a fortnight later. The time of the race was nothing special but runner-up City Of Joy won a Redcar maiden next time and the winner strode out impressively to the line.

Swiss Storm is by Frankel out of the prolific Swiss Lake, a daughter of Indian Ridge and the dam of eight winners. Plans to run him in the Racing Post Trophy were shelved, but there was certainly a hint of Group-class potential about this performance and a mile should be no problem. An early trial will give connections a guide as to where they stand but, at this stage, he appeals as one of the better outsiders. He stays with David Elsworth.

It would be significant if Andre Fabre made the trip over with **Al Wukair**. The son of Dream Ahead won a 7f maiden at Saint-Cloud in September, from two horses that were subsequently beaten three times each, before landing a 1m Listed race at Deauville in October. Emmaus and Medieval, rated 99 and 102 respectively, were fourth and fifth there, suggesting the winner ran to a mark of around 110. Al Wukair is bred to be a miler.

John Gosden has a handful of lightly-raced colts that may step up to the plate.

Cracksman, a son of Frankel, showed great tenacity to win a 1m maiden at Newmarket in October. Green early on, he looked sure to win when taking the lead on the far side rail only to be joined by Wild Tempest, who came with a swooping run down the middle of the course. To his great credit, Cracksman responded to the challenge to assert and win going away by one and a quarter lengths. A mark of 92 may underrate him.

Chessman, a son of Acclamation out of a Shamardal mare, set the pulse racing with the manner of his success on his debut in a 7f maiden at Kempton in November. Last of the 13 runners on the turn for home having missed the break, he weaved his way through the field on the bridle to quicken and win very easily by two and a quarter lengths. The form of the race has not held up – the third was beaten twice subsequently and is rated on 69

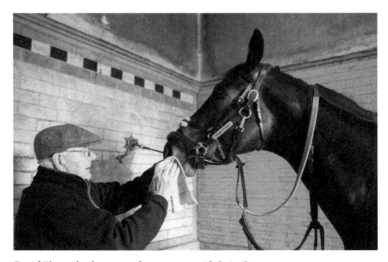

David Elsworth – has a top-class prospect with Swiss Storm

– but the winner could not have been more impressive and it's no surprise to see him hold an entry for this race.

Dreamfield won both his starts last season but he only just held on when pipping Top Score in a 7f Class 2 contest at Newmarket. As a son of Oasis Dream out of a mare by Pivotal I expect him to prove at his most effective over six furlongs.

Gosden can also call upon **Seven Heavens**, a son of Frankel who won his first two starts at Ascot and Goodwood before finishing last of seven behind Churchill in the Dewhurst. That seemed to expose his limitations and with a dam by Pivotal he is not bred to be suited to a mile.

Utmost beat Cape Byron, also a Guineas entry, by a length on his sole start at Leicester. The son of Giant's Causeway had to battle quite hard to win there, but he responded well to firm driving and is bred to get the mile.

Gosden's final entry is **Via Egnatia**, who ran well in maidens on his first two starts before striding clear to beat Never Surrender by seven lengths over a mile in October. He showed a smart turn of foot to win there, putting in a good time and clearly enjoying the fast ground and step up to a mile. I will be surprised if he does not prove effective at Pattern class level.

Aidan O'Brien has a handful of less-exposed entries that may make the line-up.

Inca Gold shaped well when second in a 7f maiden at the Curragh but he wasn't seen out again. **Intelligence Cross** won twice from seven starts but looked below this level when fourth in the Middle Park Stakes to The Last Lion. **Lancaster Bomber** showed steady improvement through the season, running second to Churchill in the Dewhurst and then runner-up in the Breeders' Cup Juvenile Turf. He should continue to figure at the highest level.

It was a surprise that **Peace Envoy** was never tried beyond six furlongs given his dam is by Dansili. He was found out at Group 1

level on his last two starts but may improve for a step up in trip.
Pedestal followed a 5f maiden win at Tipperary in May with a
fair third to Ardad in the Windsor Castle Stakes at Royal Ascot.
He was not seen out again.

Spirit Of Valor won a maiden at Naas before shaping well
when second in a Group 3 at Leopardstown in October.
Venezuela also showed promise when runner-up to Eagle Spirit
in a 1m maiden at Leopardstown in June. **War Secretary** won a
7f maiden at Dundalk in October.

Richard Hannon appears to have some promising three-year-
olds this year.

It comes as no surprise to see that **Barney Roy** will be
running in the colours of Godolphin this season. The son
of Excelebration, who is out of a Galileo mare, quickened
up smartly to beat Fujaira Bridge and subsequent winner
Crowned Eagle, now rated on 85, in a 1m maiden at Haydock in
September. Barney Roy, who is rated on 91, stays with Richard
Hannon and has the potential to prove effective at Pattern level.

Larchmont Lad made a winning debut at Sandown and then
followed up his third in a 7f Listed contest at Doncaster with a
victory in the Group 3 Tattersalls Stakes at Newmarket. After
that race the trainer said the colt would be aimed at the 2,000
Guineas and the style of his victory certainly augured well for a
step up to a mile.

Majeste has always been well regarded but Rivet held him
comfortably when they met at Doncaster in September.

Medahim showed a useful turn of foot to land a 6f maiden at
Kempton in December. Steadily away and shuffled along on the
turn for home, he quickly made up ground on the leaders to win
going away by three and a quarter lengths. Neither the form nor
the time add up to much but the son of Kodiac could not have
been more impressive.

An hour later stable companion **Son Of The Stars** won the 1m maiden by three and a quarter lengths despite racing keenly in the early stages. The son of Delegator showed a turn of foot and the runner-up won next time out.

Godolphin inevitably have a host of representatives they may want to call upon.

Big Challenge looked more a middle-distance prospect when winning a Nottingham maiden over an extended mile in November. **Boynton** beat War Decree in the Group 2 Superlative Stakes and then failed to confirm that form when third to that colt at Goodwood in July. He was not seen out again. The unraced **Dream Castle**, by Frankel out of the Dubawi filly Sand Vixen, must have shown something at home to warrant an entry here.

Leshlaa confirmed the promise shown when runner-up on his Newmarket debut in October by scooting away with a 7f maiden in a moderate time at Kempton in November. **Salsabeel** overcame signs of greenness to make a winning debut at Yarmouth in August before finding Rodaini a short head too good for him at Doncaster. **Top Score** has been busy in Meydan, winning a 7f Listed race there in February.

Hugo Palmer's **Gulliver** needs to improve considerably from his York victory in October to figure at this level. Palmer has also entered Chelmsford winner **Omeros** while **Best Of Days**, a winner of the Group 2 Royal Lodge Stakes at Newmarket in September, is bred more along Derby lines than for a Guineas.

Cape Byron, second to Utmost at Leicester, came out just eight days later to beat 12 rivals in a 7f maiden at Newmarket. Trainer Roger Varian rates the son of Shamardal quite highly but a mark of 90 reflects the task he faces to reach the top. Stable companion **Emmaus** ran fourth in a Listed contest at Deauville in October. He is bred to stay beyond a mile. **Lahore**, also trained by Varian, is an unraced son of Elusive Quality from the family of Rafha. He must have pleased at home.

Eminent lived up to his home reputation when making a winning debut for Martyn Meade at Newmarket in September. There were some fair performers behind him that day but he may be best placed trying to win a handicap off 87 before stretching to something more ambitious.

Clive Cox's **Harry Angel** won the Mill Reef Stakes in a very smart time but he is not bred to stay a mile. **Sir Dancealot** ran to a consistent level but was put in his place by Rivet in the Racing Post Trophy.

Syphax confirmed the promise shown on the home gallops when making a winning debut for Kevin Ryan at Musselburgh in July. He then took the Group 3 Acomb Stakes at York by a head from Best Of Days. Plans to run in the Breeders' Cup were shelved for this interesting prospect, who has the scope to make an impression at Group One level.

Peter Chapple-Hyam has high hopes for **Time Zone,** who won a steadily-run 7f maiden at Newmarket in September.

Ambassadorial, a winner twice at Dundalk, has shaped as if he has more to offer. Trainer Michael Halford says the colt has a very good temperament. **Apex King**, trained by Ed Dunlop, showed up well in Group 3 company last season. He is bred to improve for a trip beyond a mile.

Finally, Sir Michael Stoute would not have made a 2,000 Guineas entry for **Zainhom** without good reason. The son of Street Cry won his second start at York and was then second of ten to Best Solution in the Group 3 Autumn Stakes at Newmarket. The colt has the scope to improve and I expect him to make his mark at a high level.

CONCLUSION

No prize for imagination, but I have been keen on Churchill for the 2,000 Guineas since he won the Chesham Stakes at Royal Ascot last June. He will never be a flashy type of horse –

very much in the mould of former Ballydoyle inmates Giant's Causeway and Rock Of Gibraltar. Churchill is a grinder and galloper, who lengthens rather than quickens. As for his optimum trip, he is not really bred to stay beyond a mile even though his running style suggests he may.

Of the others, Caravaggio's participation at Newmarket will probably depend on the state of the ground and early clues gleaned from his work at home. If he stays a mile then he would be a serious threat to his stable companion.

Rivet warrants respect while it would be significant if Criquette Head-Maarek crossed the Channel with National Defense. Swiss Storm will prove popular but the two that I like from the less-exposed entries are Cracksman and Chessman, both trained by John Gosden. The former displayed a commendable attitude when winning his maiden while Chessman's turn of foot was impressive, albeit at a lowly level. Barney Roy, now with Godolphin, may be the pick of Richard Hannon's three-year-old milers while we need to respect Zainhom.

Churchill looks hard to beat but watch out for Cracksman, Chessman and Barney Roy if they do well in an early trial.

Rhododendron – sets the height of the bar

THE QIPCO 1,000 GUINEAS PREVIEW

The market for this year's 1,000 Guineas has been headed by Aidan O'Brien's **Rhododendron** for most of the winter.

The daughter of Galileo displayed both talent and courage in equal measure last season. Following an encouraging debut to finish second at the Curragh in June she overcame inexperience around a track that didn't suit her to beat 11 rivals in a 7f maiden at Goodwood in July – a race that worked out well, with subsequent winners finishing behind her.

Just less than a month later she was raised in grade for the 7f Group 2 Debutante Stakes at the Curragh. Leading entering the final furlong she battled on gamely, despite hanging right, to beat her useful stable companion Hydrangea by a head.

The following month she ran third to Intricately in the Group 1 Moyglare Stud Stakes, again not aiding her cause by hanging right.

The view that she was in need of a mile was vindicated when she went to Newmarket for the Group 1 Dubai Fillies' Mile, tackling good to firm ground for the first time since her maiden win at Goodwood. Held up off the pace, she was pushed into the lead a furlong out and ran on strongly to beat Hydrangea by two and a quarter lengths, beating her by further than she had over seven furlongs at the Curragh in August.

Rhododendron is a full sister to a Group winner over 1m 2f and a winner over a mile and a half. Her dam won three Group 1 races, twice over a mile and once over ten furlongs in the Nassau Stakes.

Rhododendron is a tough filly but she has taken a while to mature. This was evident from her tendency to hang, even in her later races, but the improvement once she was stepped up to a mile, especially on quicker ground, was there for all to see at Newmarket.

As a Group 1 winner over the Guineas course and distance, coupled with her good attitude, she is emphatically the one they have to beat. Furthermore, she is just the sort of filly her trainer handles particularly well.

This spring Charlie Appleby has already spoken in positive terms about **Wuheida**, who gave the Godolphin team such a good day when staying on gamely under firm driving to beat Rhododendron's stable companion Promise To Be True in the Group 1 Prix Marcel Boussac at Chantilly on Arc weekend.

That success came just less than two months after she beat the highly regarded and subsequent winner Spatial in a 7f maiden at Newmarket.

Everything about this filly points to her appreciating a step up in trip. It was only when meeting the rising ground that she found her stride on her debut and after being outpaced at one point in the straight at Chantilly it was stamina that saw her home.

This observation is backed up by her breeding. She is by Dubawi and her only sibling won over an extended ten furlongs. Her dam Hibaayeb, a daughter of Singspiel, won the Fillies' Mile at two and went on to win three more times at Group level, including the Ribblesdale Stakes at Royal Ascot.

The trainer says that Wuheida will probably take her chance in the Guineas but that the Oaks is viewed as her main target. Her style of racing and pedigree certainly endorse that view.

John Gosden's **Dabyah** finished third, a length behind Wuheida, in the Prix Marcel Boussac. Frankie Dettori made plenty of use of her there, leading and trying to kick for home at the distance only to get outstayed by the winner and runner-up Promise To Be True.

That run followed victories at Newmarket in July, when she

Dabyah – blessed with a turn of foot

showed a bright turn of foot to win eased down from Amabilis who was subsequently Listed placed, and then an easy nine-length victory at Newbury, where she made all.

Dabyah is a half-sister to Samtu, a winner at trips up to an extended mile and three-quarters, out of a half-sister to top performers at up to a mile and a half.

On last year's evidence she may prove more effective when held up, enabling her turn of foot to be employed to greater effect. On a strict reading of her French form she only has 2lb to find with Wuheida and, of the two, she is the more likely to be suited to a mile.

One of the most interesting once-raced fillies in the race is **Shutter Speed**.

There was plenty of talk about the filly's homework before she appeared in a 1m maiden at Yarmouth in October, and she lived up to expectations when responding to persistent urging from Frankie Dettori to beat Song Maker by a neck.

The runner-up ended the season on a mark of 82, which puts

the form into perspective, and the winner looked more of a staying type than a filly with gears. However, John Gosden was very upbeat afterwards about the daughter of Dansili's prospects and it would not take much early season chatter to see the 33/1 quickly accommodated.

Gosden also has a useful prospect named **Astronomy's Choice**. The daughter of Redoute's Choice did not catch owner Robin Geffen unawares when beating First Dance by half-a-length in a 7f maiden at Newmarket in October having shaped nicely at home.

There had been concerns beforehand that the trip would prove too sharp for the filly and, indeed, that is how it looked. Outpaced until halfway, she made relentless progress on the far side of the pack until taking the lead well inside the final furlong. She looked to need every yard of the trip and she would need to show something special in the spring to take her chance here, with the Oaks looking a more appropriate target for her.

Cashla Bay, a daughter of Fastnet Rock, has a strong speed bias to her pedigree. Despite that she stayed on well to win a 7f maiden at Newmarket in October, handling the unseasonably fast ground well. Gosden likes her, but with a dam by Pastoral Pursuits I don't fancy her chances of beating top-class opposition over a mile.

Daban, by Acclamation out of a mare by Whipper, displayed a smart turn of foot to win a 7f maiden at Kempton in November. She still appeared to have an impossible task entering the final furlong but she weaved through the field to get up close home. A rating of 75 for the third reflects the level of form but there was no denying the winner was impressive. An entry here augurs well for her prospects.

The same comment applies to **Icespire**, who won a Salisbury 7f maiden by four lengths in October. Behind early on, she was shuffled along at halfway and came with a sweeping run on the

Fair Eva – will she return to winning form?

outside looking very strong at the finish.

The third and fourth, rated 72 and 69, put the form into perspective but connections said very nice things about this daughter of Frankel after the race and she is sure to stay a mile. She looks potentially Group class.

We all got rather excited about Roger Charlton's **Fair Eva** after her victories at Haydock and Ascot.

On the second occasion, in the Princess Margaret Stakes, she came with a long run to beat Kilmah going away by four lengths recording a time just 0.08 seconds outside Henrythenavigator's track record, giving her sire Frankel his first Stakes winner.

Just under a month later she started a strongly-supported 4/11 favourite for the Group 2 Lowther Stakes at York but when asked to take the lead a furlong from home she failed to pick up, in contrast to the way she had powered away at Haydock and Ascot. She was noted as being edgy beforehand and afterwards her rider Pat Smullen said she had run a little "flat".

Fair Eva was stepped up to seven furlongs for her final start in the Shadwell Rockfel Stakes at Newmarket, a trip that was expected to suit her. Drifting right when coming to take the lead, she was soon headed by French raider Spain Burg to finish a one and a quarter lengths second.

On this occasion Pat Smullen attributed her defeat to immaturity, adding that she needs a winter to strengthen up and will be a "beautiful filly" this year. One possible area open for improvement is a step up in trip, as two of her half-sisters won over a mile while her dam comes from the family of Distant Music.

One point to make at this stage is that we don't yet know how the progeny of Frankel will train on.

There were indications from a few of his other representatives last season that they may not move forward from promising starts. This is something to monitor with his three-year-olds this spring.

Fair Eva has apparently grown and strengthened through the winter and the plan is still to aim her for the 1,000 Guineas. It will be interesting to see if she has a preliminary run anywhere as she may be best when fresh. I would not give up yet on this filly.

Sea Of Grace has joined William Haggas from John Oxx.

The daughter of Born To Sea has won her last two starts, culminating with a neck defeat of Eziyra in a 1m Group 3 contest at the Curragh in August. The feature of that performance was the way she fought back under pressure after looking beaten inside the final furlong.

John Oxx said afterwards that he felt the ground, which was officially good, may have been quicker than ideal for her. Regarding her pedigree, it augurs well for longer trips, with a distaff side that includes a Group 1 winner over a mile and three-quarters.

Haggas also has a very interesting filly named **Cristal Fizz**.

The daughter of Power beat Red Royalist by a length clear in a 6f maiden at Ascot in September having been slowly away and seemingly hopelessly out of touch for much of the race. Her chance still looked remote a furlong from home but then stamina kicked in and she won going away at the line.

The following month she beat her stable companion Glitter Girl by a neck in a 7f Listed race at Newbury, where despite persistent trouble in running from the two-furlong marker she stayed on strongly to assert close home.

Her dam, a winner over a mile and a quarter, is by Galileo so she will have no trouble staying at least a mile. Apparently she shows more on the track than she does at home, which is understandable given the way she races.

Cristal Fizz is one of the most interesting fillies in this section. If she stays beyond a mile she could be very good, with the Oaks looking a realistic target.

There are high hopes in Hamdan Al Maktoum's team that Owen Burrows will have a good season. He has been sent some of the owner's most choicely-bred two-year-olds while the stable houses a few well-regarded three-year-olds, most of them unexposed.

One of his most promising is **Talaayeb**, who is entered for both the 1,000 Guineas and Irish 1,000 Guineas along with the Irish Oaks.

The daughter of Dansili overcame a troubled run to beat what turned out to be a relatively modest field of fillies in a 7f maiden at Newmarket in September. The feature of that performance was the instant change of gear she produced inside the final furlong having travelled in arrears in the early stages of the race.

Talaayeb is a half-sister to a filly that was Group-placed over seven furlongs out of a half-sister to the owner's 1,000 Guineas winner Ghanaati and a Group 3 winner over a mile and a half that was runner-up in the Park Hill Stakes.

Talaayeb – impressed on her Newmarket debut

On that evidence she could prove effective over a mile and a quarter, perhaps even at the Oaks trip, and latest reports suggest the filly has been pleasing her trainer at home. A mark of 94 puts her within hailing distance of the best of her generation.

Aidan O'Brien is never averse to running more than one horse in a Classic, unless he feels he has a contender with outstanding claims.

One possible candidate for his support team is **Brave Anna**, who showed admirable battling qualities to beat stable companion Roly Poly in the Group 1 Cheveley Park Stakes in September.

That was a very good effort over the six-furlong trip from the daughter of War Front because her pedigree suggests she will be suited by a mile or more. Indeed, her two previous starts were over seven furlongs, finishing behind Rhododendron on both occasions. Before that she allayed her trainer's concerns about

Brave Anna – as tough as they come

the soft ground when landing the Albany Stakes at Royal Ascot.

Brave Anna is held by the favourite on various lines of form, but she appeals as a filly that could perform creditably at the highest level at a good price. Don't rush to discount her.

Roly Poly showed last season that she has the constitution to take anything her trainer asks of her.

She finished first or second in five of her eight starts, ending the campaign with a fair effort in the Breeders' Cup Juvenile Fillies' Turf at Santa Anita. There was no disgrace in her previous runs in the Lowther Stakes and Cheveley Park, finishing runner-up both times, and with a dam by Galileo she is bred to stay at least a mile.

The concern is that she is by War Front, some of whose progeny are prone not to train on at three.

Promise To Be True showed a gritty attitude to chase home Wuheida in France but then ran less well four weeks later in the Criterium International at Saint-Cloud, finishing third to Thunder Snow. She can be rated a little better than that, having taken a bump from the fading pacesetter turning for home and possibly being unsuited by the drop back to seven furlongs.

I was very taken by the way she won her first two starts at Tipperary and Leopardstown, only picking up well inside the final furlong after looking held. I have plenty of time for this filly and I love the way she came home strongly nearing the line at Chantilly. I expect her to prove one of the yard's top performers over a mile and a quarter or more, possibly with a preference for good ground or faster.

Hydrangea twice ran well against Rhododendron before ending the season by finishing last of 14 in the Breeders' Cup Juvenile Fillies' Turf. She is consistent but may struggle to confirm her superiority over her more progressive stable companions.

Rain Goddess, who beat 17 rivals in a 7f maiden at Leopardstown when trained by David Wachman, is now with Aidan O'Brien. The daughter of Galileo, who comes from the family of 1,000 Guineas winner Virginia Waters, was staying on well at the finish of her race.

Dundalk maiden winner **Winter** would not have been given an entry for this race without good reason. A mark of 89 reflects her level of form, but she comes from a good family and was going the right way last season.

Andre Fabre has made an entry for **Double Lady**.

The daughter of Stormy River easily won a 6f maiden at Maisons-Laffitte in September before running fifth to Poet's Vanity a month later at Newmarket. On form that doesn't look anything like good enough, but an entry for this race suggests her astute handler may be expecting more.

Senga, trained in France by Pascal Bary, did well to run into fourth behind Wuheida at Chantilly given how keen she was in the early stages of the race. She had won her maiden before that over a mile but there is plenty of speed in her pedigree although she will need to learn to settle if she is to fulfil her potential.

Freddy Head has a useful filly named **Alrahma**.

She won her first two starts in the summer but was then second to Lady Aurelia in the Group 1 Prix Morny at Deauville. Her dam is by Oasis Dream but there are plenty in her family who stayed a mile or more.

Her stable companion **Ettisaal**, by Dubawi and a half-sister to seven winners including Group 1 winner Tamayuz, also needs respecting. She won an extended 7f maiden in October on her only start.

Poet's Vanity may join the line-up if she pleases trainer Andrew Balding in the spring.

The daughter of Poet's Voice could not live with Wuheida when they met in August, finishing over seven lengths fourth of six, but she then hacked up by ten lengths after making all in a 7f maiden at Salisbury before beating the 101-rated Glitter Girl by a length in the Group 3 Oh So Sharp Stakes at Newmarket in October.

The concern with her is the trip. Her dam, who ran over sprint distances, is by Thatching and a half-sister to the speedy Ffestiniog. Poet's Vanity was also quite keen at Newmarket, but she has some size about her and the trainer says he had to work her with colts towards the end of last season because he didn't have a filly good enough to match her.

Andrew Balding does not overrate his horses and so monitor stable reports in the weeks leading up to the race. Whatever happens black type surely beckons for the filly.

Queen Kindly looked very smart when she beat Roly Poly and Fair Eva in the Lowther Stakes last August.

Her two wins before that had been at Catterick, but between those victories she ran a close half-length third to Brave Anna in the Albany. She may have been over the top when a one-paced fourth of six to Brave Anna in the Cheveley Park Stakes, having beaten the runner-up Roly Poly the time before at York.

Queen Kindly is by Frankel and the first foal of a mare that won at Group level as a two-year-old out of the very talented Queen's Logic, whom Mick Channon still rates as the best filly he has ever trained.

It is my belief that you sometimes have to forgive a two-year-

Queen Kindly – may be best at trips short of a mile

old a disappointing run at the back-end of the season, so I would not be quick to dismiss this filly's claims. Her trainer Richard Fahey does not get many chances to run a horse at this level, so I expect he will be keen to see her take her chance. She may, though, prove best suited to trips short of a mile.

Kevin Prendergast holds **Aneen** in high regard.

The daughter of Lawman built on the promise shown on her Leopardstown debut in September when beating 24 rivals a month later at the Curragh. She flashed her tail and needed plenty of encouragement to go about her work, but she was well clear at the line and is bred to get a mile. She will progress from this.

Intricately gave Joseph O'Brien his first Group 1 success when she pipped Hydrangea by a short head in the Moyglare Stud Stakes at the Curragh. Her next run in Santa Anita can probably be forgiven. She is bred to stay further than a mile.

Sobetsu looked the part when winning at Newmarket by ten lengths for Charlie Appleby at Newmarket in September before finishing down the field behind Rhododendron in the Fillies' Mile. As a daughter of Dubawi out of a Darshaan mare the best may not be seen of her until she tackles middle distances.

Jeremy Noseda must rate the unraced Frankel filly **La Figlia** highly to have entered her for both this race and the Irish equivalent. She is certainly bred to be special, having cost €1,800,000 as a foal. The same comment applies to the unraced **Extra Mile**, also a daughter of Frankel trained by Saeed bin Suroor.

Spiritual Lady could prove popular. Philip McBride would not get many chances to have a crack at the big time but this daughter of Pastoral Pursuits, who was well bought at £9,000 as a yearling, showed a turn of foot to win a nursery at Chelmsford off 78 and then produced a much-improved effort to win a 6f Listed race at Newmarket.

On ratings she improved by 27lb in her last two runs and her pedigree raises hopes for the step up to a mile. She is not one to discount.

Tom Dascombe reckons **Eartha Kitt** has black-type potential. The daughter of Pivotal landed a 6f maiden at Haydock on her second start but her dam won the Queen Mary Stakes and I will be very surprised if she stays a mile.

The same comment applies to Luca Cumani's **Gorgeous Noora**, a six-length winner of a Wolverhampton maiden in November. That was impressive, but her dam is by Invincible Spirit and a full sister to the sprinter Muthmir.

Isabel De Urbina showed a good attitude when beating runner-up Brogan by a neck at Ffos Las in September. The daughter of Lope De Vega needed nudging along from the start and a furlong out she was still sixth of the eight runners looking well held. It was only when her stamina kicked in that she began to stay on, getting up on the line to beat a filly that won her next race.

A mark of 80 may underrate her but her pedigree points to her requiring beyond a mile. Ralph Beckett has an excellent record with staying fillies, so don't be surprised to see her have a good year.

CONCLUSION

Aidan O'Brien appears to be controlling this race as I write, with Rhododendron supported by a strong back-up team of likely improvers. From these I took a particularly strong liking to Promise To Be True.

Much depends on how soon these fillies come to hand, but it wouldn't surprise me to see one of the more lightly-raced entries play a prominent role. John Gosden is particularly strong in this area, with Dabyah representing Group 1 form and the likes of Shutter Speed, Daban and Icespire each shaping with great potential.

Talaayeb and Poet's Vanity are interesting, while Wuheida may take in this race on the way to the Oaks.

We must not forget Fair Eva, whose time at Ascot indicates she has considerable talent.

This is difficult, but I hope to see Fair Eva return to her best. Of the others, Rhododendron and Dabyah have strong claims. Shutter Speed is the most interesting of the lightly-raced contenders.

Keep in touch

If you want to keep in touch with Marten's thoughts on a regular basis then read his free-to-view journal at:

www.martenjulian.com

or ring him on:

0906 150 1555

Selections given in the first minute
(calls charged at £1.50 a minute at all times)

Follow Marten

 @martenjulian

THE INVESTEC DERBY PREVIEW

Of the 129 horses that have been left in this year's Derby, almost a third – 39 to be precise – have not yet run while another 41 have just one appearance to their name.

Mind you, from recent times, the 2013 winner Ruler Of The World was unraced at two while being lightly-raced as a juvenile didn't stand in the way of last year's winner Harzand, who finished fifth of 15 on his sole start at two.

If **Churchill** wins then he will certainly buck the recent trend, having raced six times as a two-year-old, but he looked to need every bit of that experience, often looking outpaced early on before clicking into top gear at the business end of the race.

One thing we can be sure of is that if Churchill were to win the 2,000 Guineas his stamina and pedigree would be a constant topic of discussion in the weeks leading up to Epsom.

At the risk of being made to look foolish by mid-afternoon on the first Saturday of June, it is my view that a mile and a half will not prove to be Churchill's optimum trip. That is not to go so far as to suggest he will not stay – every horse stays, but to different degrees. It is more a case of there being other horses that are bred to be stronger over the mile and half than he is.

However, we know from recent history that any doubts on that score would not stop Aidan O'Brien and the team from letting him take his chance at Epsom. These days, defeat in the Derby for a colt that has proved himself as top class over a mile or a mile and a quarter does not appear to impact adversely on a horse's market value at stud.

Yet Churchill's pedigree does raise serious doubts about his likely effectiveness over middle distances.

Churchill is the second foal of Meow, a daughter of Storm Cat who only raced five times, all at two, winning a maiden at Tipperary and a Listed race at the Curragh. She also finished second in the Queen Mary Stakes and ended her career in the Flying Childers, coming home last of 12. She never raced beyond five furlongs and looked pure speed.

Meow is a half-sister to two winners over a mile and a little further while her dam, Airwave, won the Temple Stakes and Cheveley Park although she did win a Group 2 over a mile.

As illustrated in the 2,000 Guineas preview, Churchill runs in the manner of a colt who will appreciate a mile and beyond. He has looked most at ease in the closing stages of a race, but there is no getting away from the evidence of his pedigree which strongly suggests he is bred along miling lines.

My view is that he will probably prove effective over a little beyond a mile – perhaps a mile and a quarter – but I would not fancy his chances of staying a strongly-run mile and a half at Epsom.

O'Brien has, inevitably, plenty of other less-exposed types he can call upon.

Capri has few doubts on that score. He looked a staying type when winning three times last summer, notably responding to strong driving to beat stable companion Yucatan in the Group 2 Beresford Stakes at the Curragh in September. He ran well when third to Waldgeist over ten furlongs in the Group 1 Criterium de Saint-Cloud in October, doing strong late work up the centre of the track. His dam, Dialafara, won over an extended mile and a half and comes from a family of middle-distance winners.

Capri is a tough and likeable colt who can be relied upon to give his running. He is untried on ground faster than soft, but as a son of Galileo that should not be a problem. He may lack a gear but at 20/1 he would make some appeal if Epsom was part of the plan.

Capri – exceptionally tough

Yucatan, by Galileo out of the hugely talented Six Perfections, should stay the mile and a half. He found Capri three-quarters of a length too good for him at the Curragh in September and then Rivet beat him in the Racing Post Trophy at Doncaster a month later.

Yucatan clearly has ground to find but his breeding points to improvement for a step up in trip.

Sir John Lavery won a 1m maiden at Gowran Park on his second start by seven lengths but his dam is by Fusaichi Pegasus, who tends to inject speed rather than stamina into a pedigree.

Exemplar ran third to Capri in the Beresford Stakes, looking one-paced at the finish. He is held on that form but he is out of a Linamix mare and has a pedigree packed with stamina. Watch for him over a distance of ground in the autumn, with the English or Irish St Leger possible targets.

Other Ballydoyle colts to watch for are the unraced **Air Supremacy** and **Wisconsin**. Of those that have run **Auckland**, third to Sir John Lavery at Gowran, Leopardstown winner **Cliffs Of Moher**, **Spanish Steps**, who showed promise behind Titus in October, and Dundalk winner **War Secretary** are worth noting.

There are no stamina doubts about **Waldgeist**, who has a rock-solid middle-distance pedigree.

Andre Fabre's son of Galileo is out of a daughter of Monsun who is a half-sister to St Leger winner Masked Marvel from the family of a German Derby winner. He won the 1m 2f Criterium de Saint-Cloud despite being short of room early in the straight, producing a smart turn of foot to beat Best Solution and Capri.

The concern with him is that his form before that, when third to Frankuus at Chantilly in October, does not hold up while Best Solution has been well beaten in Meydan in February.

Fabre has a less-exposed contender named **Franz Schubert**. The son of Dansili is a half-brother to 1m 4f winner Summer School out of a half-sister to 1m 4f Group 1 winner Anabaa Blue from the family of Urban Sea. The colt won a 9f maiden at Chantilly in October with something in hand.

Pharaonic could be interesting. The son of Dansili won what turned out to be a weak 1m maiden at Saint-Cloud in October but as a half-brother to the top-class French Derby winner New Bay he is bred to thrive over middle distances.

Fabre has also entered **Last Kingdom**, a son of Frankel who ran second in maiden company at Clairefontaine and Saint-Cloud. He needs to improve but is bred to do so.

William Haggas has a strong team of three-year-old colts this season, headed by **Rivet**.

His sire Fastnet Rock has got winners over a mile and a half – Fascinating Rock is one of the best of them – while his dam Starship is a daughter of Galileo. She has produced winners at up to a mile and a quarter, including Group 3 winner Alexander Pope.

Rivet has ground to find with Churchill from their meeting in the Dewhurst Stakes but he ended the season with a victory in the Racing Post Trophy, looking well suited to the mile. My view is that Rivet will stay the mile and a half without being good enough to win at this level.

William Haggas must be pleased with his crop of three-year-olds judging by the handful of other Epsom entries.

They include Lingfield all-weather winner **Across Dubai**, the unraced Galileo colt **Call To Mind**, who is owned by the Queen, a Teofilo half-brother to seven winners named **Daawy**, two sons of Frankel named **Elyaasaat** and **The Grand Visir**, a colt by High Chaparral named **Humble Hero** and **Transatlantic**, a son of Galileo.

John Gosden has one of the strongest entries in the race.

Golden Horn had to be supplemented in his year and **Tartini**, a son of Giant's Causeway and a half-brother to St Leger winner Lucarno and others who won over a distance of ground, may also be supplemented if he has a good spring. Although equipped

John Gosden – holds a strong hand in all the Classics

with a tongue-tie for his debut at Nottingham, and starting at 25/1, his half-length victory did not surprise the trainer.

Stable companion **Cracksman** is also without an entry. The son of Frankel showed a good attitude to win a maiden at Newmarket but his dam is by Pivotal and he is not sure to stay a mile and a half.

Golden Horn landed the Derby two years ago on the back of a Nottingham maiden victory at two and he has a few colts with similar profiles entered this year.

Azam won a 1m 2f all-weather maiden at Kempton on his third start but a mark of 87 reflects the level of the form. **Crowned Eagle** won an extended 1m maiden at Nottingham despite hanging left. **Face The Facts**, with a sound middle-distance pedigree, ran second to Youmkin at Nottingham.

Other entries from the yard include **Pealer**, runner-up in a 9f maiden at Goodwood in October, **Percy B Shelley**, a son of Archipenko who is evidently thought rather better than his fifth of 11 in an extended 1m 1f maiden at Wolverhampton represents, Nottingham maiden third **Wasatch Range** and the Frankel colt **Weekender**, who started even-money when fourth on his debut at Haydock in October.

From his crop of unraced entries look out for **Erdogan**, a son of Frankel and the third foal of Dar Re Mi, **Great Sound**, by Galileo from the family of Cheveley Park winner Wannabe Grand, and **Peterport**, a son of Nathaniel and a three-parts brother to Gallipot and half-brother to four other winners.

There was plenty of talk about Sir Michael Stoute's **Mirage Dancer** before he landed some hefty bets in a 7f maiden at Doncaster in October.

The son of Frankel needed firm driving from Ryan Moore to beat a colt who ended the season an eight-race maiden. The colt is out of a half-sister to Dansili, Banks Hill and other top-class performers but on the book his status owes more to his reputation than the bare evidence of his form.

Crystal Ocean, by Sea The Stars, is from the family of Hillstar, Crystal Capella and last year's slightly disappointing Crystal Zvezda. He shaped quite well when second to Warrior's Spirit in a modestly run 7f maiden at Newbury in September. He comes from a family the trainer knows very well and I gather he is considered one of the yard's better middle-distance three-year-old prospects.

Pivoine, a very comfortable winner of a 1m maiden at Kempton on his second start, is the first foal of a daughter of Montjeu who won over 1m 5f. He comes from the family of Melbourne Cup winner Fiorente, who started his career with Stoute, and the top-class Islington. This promising colt has Group-class potential.

Elucidation stepped up from his promising debut to beat Sporting Times in a 7f maiden at Leicester in September. His pedigree is a blend of speed and stamina, by Oasis Dream out of a daughter of Silver Hawk related to Kris Kin. He is rated on 88 but his presence here suggests the trainer is expecting more from him.

The Queen's **Frontispiece** beat Make Time, a winner on his next start, by a nose on his debut in a 7f maiden at Ascot in September. That trip on good to firm ground might have been sharp enough for this son of Shamardal, whose dam is from the family of the owner's top-class middle-distance filly Phantom Gold.

Karawaan, by Sea The Stars out of a daughter of Cadeaux Genereux, will improve on his fifth of nine in a Yarmouth maiden in September. He was very green there.

Sir Michael does not make frivolous entries so we need to monitor the progress of his unraced **Abjar**, a son of Nathaniel out of Group 1 winner Kinnaird. There is no shortage of stamina in his pedigree.

Dermot Weld's **Titus** kept on well to beat 14 rivals in a 1m Leopardstown maiden in October. His dam is from a family of middle-distance performers and the trainer said he would like to run the colt in a trial this spring. A mark of 84 for Clongowes, who finished third, puts the form into perspective but this is a big colt with the scope to improve.

Weld has also entered the unraced **Neptune**, a full brother to Irish 1,000 Guineas winner Nightime and winners at up to two miles. **Haripour**, a distant second to Sir John Lavery at Gowran in October, is also entered. **Rich History**, a half-brother to Free Eagle and Sapphire, will need to make considerable improvement from his two runs last season to match their ability.

Godolphin are well represented at the entry stage with horses from the yards of Saeed bin Suroor and Charlie Appleby.

Alaik, by New Approach, ran third to John Gosden's possible Derby candidate Tartini in an extended mile maiden at Nottingham. **Alqamar** is bred to stay long trips but after three runs earning a mark of 76 he has a mountain to climb. **Big Challenge** won an extended 1m maiden at Nottingham but the time was slow and the form doesn't add up to a great deal. **First Nation** was given a mark of 83 after winning an extended 1m maiden at Wolverhampton in November. **Sea Skimmer** shaped quite well in fifth on his Newbury debut in October as did **Tamleek** when third at Yarmouth in October.

One of Godolphin's best prospects is **Youmkin**, who showed a fair turn of foot to beat Face The Facts in a very slowly run extended 1m maiden at Nottingham in October.

Godolphin's unraced contenders include **Benbatl**, a son of Dubawi from the family of Sarrsar, **Dubai Thunder**, who also has an entry for the 2,000 Guineas, **Forever Song**, a half-brother to four winners including 2m winner Whispering Gallery, **Glassy Waters**, a son of Distorted Humor from the family of a UAE 1,000 Guineas and Oaks winner, and **Zamfir**, a son of

New Approach out of a useful German mare.

Godolphin stepped in to acquire **Atty Persse** after he responded to quiet urgings to win a 1m maiden at Sandown in September. They had a line to the form through runner-up Hamada, who won his next race and ended his season on a mark of 87. The colt had shown plenty of talent at home before his debut and as a son of Frankel out of a mare by Norse Dancer he should stay beyond a mile. He may well become the team's main hope for Epsom.

The Godolphin silks are also carried by **Dubai Sand**, who was nominated for a spring trial by trainer Jim Bolger after he beat Diodorus in a 1m 1f Listed race at Leopardstown in October. This was an improved performance from the son of Teofilo after a couple of runs at the Curragh but he is not certain to stay a mile and a half.

There are a number of unraced colts from a variety of sources that have been given entries.

They include **Achibueno**, a son of Dansili with a sound middle-distance pedigree trained by Alain De Royer-Dupre, **Sheerlar**, by Shamardal and also trained by De Royer-Dupre, **Al Galayel**, a son of Zoffany trained by Luca Cumani, **Fayyadh**, by Dubawi trained by Jean-Claude Rouget, **Impact Point**, by Deep Impact trained by Andrew Balding, **Petitioner**, by Dansili trained by Roger Charlton and **Towie**, a son of Sea The Stars trained by Hughie Morrison.

Others to note are David Simcock's **Captor**, a son of Frankel out of a full sister to Irish Derby third Jan Vermeer, David O'Meara's **Sunrize**, a son of Azamour related to hurdle winners, and **Yamarhaba Malayeen**, by Rip Van Winkle out of a 1m 1f Group 3 winner.

Morrison has also made a Derby entry for **Temple Church**, a son of Lawman out of an unraced half-sister to French St Leger winner Allegretto from the family of Last Second. This colt has

Atty Persse – now owned by Godolphin

one of the stoutest pedigrees in the field and I already have him marked down as a possible St Leger prospect. He is one to follow, especially over a distance of ground.

Luca Cumani has entered narrow 1m Lingfield maiden winner **Manangatang** and **Red Label**, a son of Dubawi who appeared to relish the extended mile when winning a maiden at Leicester in October. This colt, who comes from the family of world-class racemare Goldikova, is sure to pay his way over middle distances. He is one to note.

Commander, a Frankel half-brother to seven winners including a 3m hurdle winner, will be improving on his eighth of 14 for Roger Varian at Newbury in October. Stable companion **Solomon's Bay** was disappointing when last of 10 to Best Solution at Newmarket.

Count Octave, third of 10 in a 9f maiden at Goodwood in October, is bred to stay well. This half-brother to Elidor is closely related to Irish Derby winner Treasure Beach but he will need to settle better than he did on his debut if he is to fulfil his potential.

De Royer-Dupre has made an entry for the Aga Khan's **Devamani**, who finished third in an extended 7f maiden at Saint-Cloud in November.

Hugo Palmer has made entries for **Escobar** and **Manchego**.

The former showed a turn of foot to win his first two starts, both at Newbury, but was then put in his place in a Group 3 contest at Newmarket. Manchego, a son of Lope De Vega, ran second to the well-regarded Cape Byron at Newmarket in

Hugo Palmer – set for another good season

October. Despite being out of a Green Desert mare he has a half-brother that stayed two miles, so middle distances may not be beyond him.

Owen Burrows has a strong influx of promising sorts this season and **Okool** was very unfortunate not to win both his starts last season. The son of Cape Cross was seriously hampered at both Doncaster and Newmarket, both times over a mile. His dam is a half-sister to a German Listed 1m 6f winner so he is bred to stay very well.

Ralph Beckett has taken charge of **Intern**, a son of Rip Van Winkle who ran third to Capri in a Listed contest at Tipperary when trained by David Wachman. A three-parts brother to 3m chase winner Expanding Universe, he is bred to relish middle distances.

Richard Hannon's **Giant's Treasure** left a good impression when making a winning debut in a 7f maiden at Wolverhampton in March. That was a most encouraging start for the son of Shamardal as he is bred to stay much further.

CONCLUSION

If Churchill wins the 2,000 Guineas he will become a short-priced favourite for the Derby. My view is that he will be allowed to take his chance at Epsom, as this is the policy Aidan O'Brien tends to adopt with his Guineas winners if he thinks they have a chance of staying the trip.

Capri makes the stronger appeal, because his breeding and style of racing suggest he is sure to stay. At 20/1 he could represent fair value but it would help to know that the Derby was in the long-term plan. Stable companion Exemplar may also creep into the picture.

Anything Andre Fabre sends over would command respect while it will be of great significance if John Gosden supplements Tartini or Cracksman. If either colt is entered for an established trial, notably the Dante Stakes at York, then that would be a strong pointer. Of the two Tartini has the stronger middle-distance pedigree.

Sir Michael Stoute's Crystal Ocean and Pivoine are interesting while Youmkin and Atty Persse look the best of Godolphin's prospects at this stage. Hughie Morrison's Temple Church is a colt I like, but probably more for the autumn.

Capri has an appealing profile and at 20/1 there is some value. Tartini and Atty Persse are others to watch for.

If you want to keep in touch with Marten's thoughts on a regular basis then read his free-to-view journal at:

www.martenjulian.com

or ring him on:

0906 150 1555

Selections given in the first minute

(calls charged at £1.50 a minute at all times)

 @martenjulian

THE INVESTEC
OAKS PREVIEW

*Please note that the following preview has been written without
the benefit of entries. If you intend to have an interest on any of
the horses mentioned, please either ensure your bet is 'with a run'
or await the entry stage in April.*

As I have noted before in past editions of the *Dark Horses*,
the Oaks is the most difficult of the first four Classics to assess
because it can be won by a filly that is unexposed or even
unraced in her first season. The situation is further complicated
by having to write this preview without the benefit of entries.

Taghrooda was selected in 2014 on the strength of her
promising maiden victory at two and what I deemed to be a
rock-solid middle-distance pedigree. The previous year Talent,
winner of her second start as a juvenile, had a similar profile.
By contrast, last year's Oaks winner Minding was thoroughly
exposed and proved to be in a league apart from her rivals.

Minding's class probably got her home at Epsom – her best
performances came at a mile and a mile and a quarter – but
generally the Oaks winner has a pedigree strongly endowed with
stamina and that will be the focus of interest in what follows.

There can't be much doubt that if **Rhododendron** wins or
runs well in the 1,000 Guineas then she will be aimed at the
Oaks, perhaps taking the Irish Guineas on the way.

The daughter of Galileo is a full sister to winners over 1m 2f
and 1m 4f out of a speedily-bred triple Group 1 winner at up to
1m 2f. She settled well in her races last season and was coming
away comfortably at the finish of the Fillies' Mile in October.

One of the other likely market leaders for the race is **Coronet**,
a daughter of Dubawi out of the Darshaan mare Approach.

Her dam, who won up to 1m 2f, is a half-sister to French

Guineas winner Aussie Rules. At stud she has produced five winners including 1m 2f Group 2 winner and St Leger second Midas Touch and 1m 2f winner Streetcar To Stars.

Coronet won both her starts last season, despite starting slowly each time. The first came in an extended 1m maiden at Leicester, where she needed to be nudged along before taking the lead a furlong out. The form was nothing special with Castellated, who was one and a half lengths back in third, now rated on 73.

Just over a month later John Gosden ran Coronet in the Listed Zetland Stakes over 1m 2f at Newmarket. Held up off the pace after another slow start, she made steady progress on the outside of the field before taking the lead inside the final furlong. At the line she was a neck ahead of her 97-rated stable companion Cunco.

The trainer said afterwards that Coronet would be aimed at the Musidora Stakes on her way to Epsom for the Oaks.

With an official rating of 99 Coronet is assessed 17lb inferior to Rhododendron, but she is a very different type of filly. The former had the class and pace to win at Group 1 level at two, while Coronet is more a middle-distance prospect who required every yard of the trip when winning the Zetland Stakes over Newmarket's mile and a quarter.

Of the two I expect her to prove the more natural stayer, but there is no evidence yet that she has a turn of foot. Mind you, that is not always required to win an Epsom Classic.

The filly with the strongest credentials is **Wuheida**.

She showed last season that she has both class and pace, having won a useful 7f maiden on her debut at Newmarket in August and then landing the Group 1 Prix Marcel Boussac from Promise To Be True and Dabyah, both top-class performers, at Chantilly on Arc day.

Her trainer Charlie Appleby already views her more as an Oaks filly, which is in accordance with the evidence of her

Wuheida – the Oaks looks her natural target

pedigree. As a daughter of Dubawi out of a high-class middle-distance winning daughter of Singspiel there should be no doubts about her effectiveness over a mile and a half.

Rated on 114 she is just 2lb adrift of the favourite yet of the two she has the stronger middle-distance pedigree.

Of the three fillies at the head of the market Wuheida has the soundest credentials on grounds of form, pedigree and class.

Sobetsu also has middle-distance claims.

The daughter of Dubawi is out of Lake Toya, a daughter of Darshaan who is a half-sister to a 1m 3f winner from the family of Oaks and Irish 1,000 Guineas winner Imagine. It may be best to overlook her 15-length defeat by Rhododendron in the Fillies' Mile, as she became unbalanced in the dip and may not have been suited to the quick ground.

As you will be aware from my 1,000 Guineas preview I have a great liking for **Promise To Be True**.

The daughter of Galileo looked to be crying out for a step up in trip when finishing with a flourish to chase home Wuheida in

Promise To Be True – immensely likeable and tough

the Marcel Boussac and there may have been an excuse for her at Saint-Cloud four weeks later. As stated earlier she was doing her best work very late on when winning her first two starts and with a distaff side related to Derby winner Dr Devious and Oaks winner Dancing Rain everything points to her appreciating a mile and a half.

Aidan O'Brien will have plenty of options come the first week of June, but I expect this tough filly to feature high in the pecking order for an Oaks, if not at Epsom then for the Irish Oaks at the Curragh.

Hydrangea has a pound or two to find with Rhododendron and despite being out of a speedy daughter of Pivotal her full brothers, The United States and Buonarroti, won over trips just beyond a mile and a half.

Rain Goddess, now with O'Brien from David Wachman, is less certain to get the trip, with a distaff side linked predominantly to milers.

Brave Anna did exceptionally well to win the Cheveley Park Stakes given that her pedigree has as much stamina as speed. Her dam is by Sadler's Wells and is a half-sister to 1m 2f winner

The Bogberry. At stud she has produced the full sister Hit It A Bomb, who stayed a mile well.

Roly Poly may also stay further than last season's impressions might suggest as her dam Misty For Me is by Galileo and won at Group 1 level up to a mile and a quarter. I think it unlikely she will get a mile and a half, but it's not impossible.

Unraced fillies to note from Ballydoyle are **Longing** and **Music Box**.

Joseph O'Brien's **Intricately** is also a likely stayer. She is by Fastnet Rock out of a half-sister by Galileo to Rock Of Gibraltar. Her form falls within 5 or 6lb of the best of her generation.

Unraced stable companion **On Ice**, a full sister to the talented but ultimately disappointing Kingsbarns, is a name to note. **Detailed**, third on her sole start at two, is also quite nice.

Crimson Rock, winner of a 1m maiden at Newbury in October, is bred to stay well.

The daughter of Fastnet Rock, who cost $1,000,000 as a yearling, is a three-parts sister to the top-class Group 1 middle-distance winner Peeping Fawn out of a daughter of Sadler's Wells.

She did well to win at Newbury, having swerved and run green in the early stages before taking up the running inside the final furlong to win a little snugly. Her trainer, Ralph Beckett, won the same Newbury maiden race in 2012 with subsequent Oaks runner-up Secret Gesture.

Beckett has another possible contender named **Gemina**. The daughter of Holy Roman Emperor is from the family of top-class stayer Fame And Glory but she needs to improve on her second in Listed class at Salisbury, as reflected in her mark of 89.

Stable companion **Rich Legacy** won the Group 2 May Hill Stakes but couldn't handle her last two starts in Group 1 company. She comes from a strong German staying family so the trip won't pose her a problem.

Isabel De Urbina, also trained by Beckett, looked an out-and-out stayer when plugging away to beat Brogan on easy ground at Ffos Las in September. She is hardly likely to make for pretty viewing but as a daughter of Lope De Vega out of a mare by Daylami she should stay a mile and a half without problem.

Talaayeb could prove a strong contender if she stays this far.

The daughter of Dansili quickened discernibly to win a 7f maiden at Newmarket having taken a while to find her stride. She won in the manner of a filly that will stay further and her bottom line – out of a mare that ran second in the Park Hill Stakes, from the family of Nashwan – is very encouraging in that respect. It will be interesting to see where she is pitched in the spring.

Eziyra, who won a Group 3 for Dermot Weld on her final start of the season, is a product of one of the Aga Khan's most successful staying families. She is a third foal half-sister to 1m 4f winner Enzani out of a middle-distance winning half-sister to Ascot Gold Cup winners Estimate and Enzeli and Irish Oaks and French Leger winner Ebadiyla.

Despite that strong bias towards stamina her trainer views her more as a Guineas filly, so that may be her early target. She will then have the option of stepping up in trip if she suggests that she can handle it.

The trainer also has good things to say about **Mujaazy**. The daughter of New Approach ran well against Capri on her second start and then beat Bound over a mile in August. From the family of Nayef and Nashwan, she is expected to prove useful over middle distances.

The trainer may also make an entry for the unraced **Espoir D'Soleil**, a daughter of Galileo and a half-sister to seven winners including Group 1 winner Casual Conquest. **Aldhara**, the third foal of Irish 1,000 Guineas winner Bethrah, **Harrana**, by New Approach from the family of last year's Derby winner Harzand,

Hazama, also from the family of Harzand, and **Tocco D'Amore**, a €2,000,000 half-sister to Echo Of Light from the family of top racemare Salsabil, are others to note from the yard.

Terrakova, a daughter of Galileo, is the second foal of the world-class mare Goldikova. She won a 1m 1f maiden for Freddy Head by three and a half lengths at Chantilly in November. Connections may prefer to keep her at home, but if she were to run at Epsom I would not expect the trip to pose a problem.

John Gosden will inevitably have a handful of strong entries.

Dabyah showed plenty of pace last season, notably when trying to make all in the Prix Marcel Boussac. Yet as a half-sister to Samtu, a winner over an extended mile and three-quarters from the family of French 1m 4f Listed winner Reverie Solaire, she is bred to stay beyond a mile.

She is probably considered more a Guineas filly at this stage, but if she settles I see no reason why she should not stay the Oaks trip.

Enable, by Nathaniel out of a 1m 2f winning full sister to an extended 1m 4f Group 2 winner, looks very interesting. She had a filly rated 72 back in third when winning a 1m maiden at Newcastle on her sole outing last season. She is likely to be placed to run in an early trial.

John Gosden may also aim **Astronomy's Choice** at a trial.

She looked to require every yard of the trip when winning a 7f maiden in October and her pedigree points to her relishing a distance of ground. Her dam is a three-parts sister to 1m 7f winner Pacifique from the family of 1m 4f Group 2 winner Pongee and Irish Oaks winner Chicquita. In the circumstances she did well to win over seven furlongs at two.

There are mixed message from the pedigree of **Shutter Speed**.

The Yarmouth winner is by Dansili but her dam is by the sprinter Oasis Dream. Her first foal, though, did win over 1m 6f. Shutter Speed took her time to win over a mile in the soft

Astronomy's Choice – gets up close home for a winning debut

ground, so I expect her to stay further, possibly being seen to greater effect on better ground.

Daban looks likely to be most effective over a mile, perhaps a little further, while Salisbury maiden winner **Icespire** is a three-parts sister to 1m 4f winner Ventoux. She may get the Oaks trip.

Sea Of Grace, trained by William Haggas, may get a mile and a half. Her dam won over the trip and two of her foals won at a mile and a quarter.

Stable companion **Cristal Fizz** does not have as strong a staying pedigree as you would imagine from the way she won at Ascot and Newbury. It took her an eternity to get going on both occasions, but as a daughter of Power out of a half-sister to the speedy Hitchens and Tanzeel she is not overendowed with stamina. If she does stay beyond a mile then I expect her to prove very useful.

Roger Varian may make an entry for the stoutly-bred **Serenada**, a daughter of Azamour out of a Daylami mare closely related to Conduit. She shaped well when third to Crimson Rock at Newbury.

Jeremy Noseda likes **Tranquil Star**, an unraced daughter of Galileo out of a Group 1 middle-distance winner in New Zealand.

I would not expect **Fair Eva** to be asked to race in the Oaks, even though it is not beyond the realms of possibility that she might stay beyond a mile.

CONCLUSION

It is entirely possible that the winner of this year's Oaks has not even been mentioned in this preview. However, at this stage, there appears to be a particularly strong clutch of possible contenders, both from the exposed and less-exposed divisions.

The three at the head of the market have very sound claims – Rhododendron, Coronet and Wuheida, while I would also have great respect for Dabyah. The four set a high level for the unexposed fillies to aim at.

Promise To Be True has something to find on form but she is very game and I really took to the way she finished her races. She could creep up and surprise a few of her more established rivals.

From the less-exposed ranks I like Astronomy's Choice and Talaayeb.

This is challenging, but Promise To Be True, Coronet and Wuheida are the three that make the most appeal, with marginal preference for the first named.

INDEX